INSIGHT GUIDES

EXPLORE
VENICE

CONTENTS

ARCHITECTURE FANS

Highlights include St Mark's Basilica (route 1), Grand Canal palaces (route 2), the Gesuati (route 7), San Giorgio Maggiore and Il Redentore (route 8) and the Gothic Frari (route 9).

RECOMMENDED ROUTES FOR...

ART BUFFS

Don't miss the Accademia (route 3), the Guggenheim and Punta della Dogana (route 7), masterpieces by Bellini, Titian and Tintoretto (route 9) and the Querini-Stampalia (route 5).

CHILDREN

Head up the bell tower in Piazza San Marco (route 1); take a boat trip on the Grand Canal (route 2); sample mouth-watering ice creams on the Zattere (route 7); or have fun on the beach or on a bike around the Lido (route 13).

FILM FANS

Admire Grand Canal palaces from *Casino Royale* (route 2), pay homage to *Death in Venice* at the Lido (route 13) and visit Castello (routes 5 and 6) and San Polo (route 9), where *Don't Look Now* was filmed.

FOODIES

Try Cannaregio (route 11) for traditional *bacari*; the Rialto (route 10) for authentic bars and cosy inns; and the backstreets of Castello, San Polo or Dorsoduro for funkier, reinvented *bacari* (routes 5, 6, 7 and 9).

MUSIC LOVERS

Tour La Fenice (route 4) and look out for concerts in the Scuole (route 9), La Salute (route 7), the Frari (route 9) and Santa Maria Formosa (route 5) or palaces, from Ca' Rezzonico (route 2) to Querini-Stampalia (route 5).

ROMANTICS

Lap up the Grand Canal on a late-night ferry (route 2); have dinner on a lagoon island: Venissa on Burano (route 12); take an atmospheric gondola ride; or simply fall for Venice in the winter mists.

SHOPPERS

West of San Marco (route 4) is good for designer wares, while the Rialto (route 10) is great for food. For Venetian crafts, try Santa Croce (route 9) for masks, Cannaregio (route 11), and Murano (route 12) for glass.

INTRODUCTION

An introduction to Venice's geography, customs and culture, plus illuminating background information on cuisine, history and what to do when you're there.

The entrance to the Grand Canal

EXPLORE VENICE

More like a stage set than a city, Venice has captivated visitors for centuries. 'La Serenissima' is one of the wonders of the world. This guide reveals the show–stopping sights and secret corners of this gloriously mesmerising place.

Endlessly portrayed by writers, painters and philosophers, Venice is a canvas for every clichéd fantasy. Almost everyone who is anyone has been there. As a result, Venice can play cultural one-upmanship better than most cities. The Romantics were rewarded with a feeling of having come too late to a world too old. The Victorians saw Venice as dying, while contemporary doom-mongers now seek to bury the city anew. Although entombment by the sea would show symmetry, this resilient city rejects such neat scenarios, with new life and vitality being pumped through its veins.

The only city in the world built entirely on water, Venice is no mere fantasy land, but a superior theme park that can uplift the spirit. You can sleep in Tchaikovsky's bed or wake up in cavernous apartments that once welcomed princes and doges, Henry James and Hemingway. For romance, you can literally walk in Casanova's footsteps; for Baroque passion, succumb to a Vivaldi concerto in Vivaldi's church, or savour the gondoliers' songs that inspired Verdi and Wagner. If feeling adventurous, explore the world of Marco Polo in his home city, bargain in the Rialto with latter-day merchants of Venice, or pick up the cobalt-blue cabbages that sent Elizabeth David into culinary raptures.

If feeling contemplative, you can ponder the passing of time with Proust's ghost in Caffè Florian. If fortunate, you can capture Canaletto's views with your camera or see Titian's painting in the church it was designed for. If gregarious, you can savour the gossip and Martinis at Harry's Bar, Hemingway's favourite. The morbid can play roulette in Wagner's death chamber, now the city casino, or quietly contemplate death on Thomas Mann's Lido.

For more than a millennium, the Republic of Venice used all its power to repel unwelcome invaders. Today, one of the greatest ever maritime powers has become one of the greatest ever tourist attractions.

NAVIGATING THE CITY

Venice is divided into six **sestieri** (districts), with very different characters. This guide presents their particularities, outlines a vaporetto trip along the Grand Canal and transports you to the islands in the lagoon.

San Giorgio Maggiore boasts a spectacular setting

As well as encompassing the architectural glories, we unpick the city neighbourhoods, including an insider's take on lesser-known corners, from bohemian bars to authentic crafts shops. Despite its watery character, Venice is made for walking: you can mostly weave your way around on foot, with brief forays on ferries that circle the city or whisk you to the outer reaches of the lagoon.

Pounding the streets

Venice is a magical city to explore on foot. Leave behind the San Marco crowds and you soon find yourself in a warren of narrow alleys *(calli)*, moody canals and secret *campi* (squares). Wherever you go there are waterfront cafés, or tiny *bacari* (bars), ideal for a Prosecco and a plate of seafood *cicchetti*, the Venetian equivalent of tapas.

NEIGHBOURHOODS

No matter your intention, you are inexorably drawn back to Piazza San Marco, directed by the bossy yellow *'per San Marco'* signs that mark the main thoroughfares. It is no hardship to return. The beautifully proportioned square that Napoleon termed 'the finest drawing room in Europe' is home to the great Basilica, the Doge's Palace and gracious cafés.

Castello, San Polo and Santa Croce

To the north of San Marco lies Castello, the largest *sestiere*, with monumental Venice gradually giving way to domestic Venice, as dark alleys open on to bright, bustling squares. The area is home to several major churches, as well as the Arsenale, the great military and naval complex founded in the 12th century, and the Biennale gardens, home to the contemporary art and architecture shows that give Venice a modern edge.

San Polo and Santa Croce are adjoining districts that encompass the labyrinthine Rialto market, with its boisterous bars, and the iconic Rialto Bridge that, with St Mark's, is the city's mercantile heart and great pulsating hub. Nearby is the Frari, the greatest of all Venetian Gothic churches.

Cannaregio and Dorsoduro

Cannaregio offers a slice of everyday Venice, from domestic vignettes of washing draped above decrepit palaces to lovely churches on back canals, culminating in the haunting Jewish Ghetto. Chic Dorsoduro is the artiest *sestiere*, with beguiling walks along the Zattere quayside, and bohemian backwaters counterpointed by the grand-standing art and architecture of La Salute basilica, the Accademia gallery and the Guggenheim collection of modern art.

Islands of the lagoon

Frequent ferries make the mysterious islands easy to reach. Murano is famous for glassmaking, Burano for colourful fishermen's cottages, and

Gondolas at dusk

Torcello for its cathedral, the oldest monument in the lagoon. Giudecca, an island undergoing a rebirth, is home to Il Redentore church, a Palladian masterpiece, and to glamorous hotels and good-value *trattorie*. San Giorgio Maggiore is the site of a famous Benedictine monastery; while the Lido, a long strip of land between the city and the Adriatic, glories in its role as a superior film set.

The festive year

Chances are there will be some celebration during your stay. After the pre-Lenten carnival extravaganza the next celebrations honour the city's patron saint, St Mark (25 April). Venice also plays host to water festivals redolent of the pomp and pageantry of the Republic, beginning with the Vogalonga rowing marathon in May. The grandest water pageant is September's Historical Regatta. The calvacade of boats winds its way from the Giardini quarter to Ca' Foscari on the Grand Canal, where prizes are presented by dignitaries on a ceremonial barge. The Biennale, a highlight of the international art calendar, is held from May-November in odd years, with the Biennale dell'Architettura held in intervening years. Other key dates include the Feast of the Redeemer (see page 63); the Film Festival (see page 23); and November's Festa della Madonna della Salute, giving thanks for the city's survival from the plague.

VENICE IN PERIL

The biggest watery threat to Venice is *acqua alta* (high water), a seasonal phenomenon caused by south-easterly Sirocco winds and high tides. In autumn and winter, duckboards are a familiar sight in Piazza San Marco and other low-lying areas of central Venice. Work is nearing completion on the controversial MOSE project (www.mosevenezia.eu), the mobile flood barriers (nicknamed after the New Testament prophet who parted the waves) that will close off the lagoon during the high tides. Progress has been painfully slow, hampered by shortage of state funds and protests by environmental campaigners. The project is currently 80 percent complete, and the inflatable barriers, which will rise up from the seabed during seriously high tides, were successfully tested for the first time in 2013. The latest estimated date for completion is 2016 (the first deadline was 1995).

MOSE has so far cost over £5bn and debate rages over its cost, efficacy and environmental impact. At best it is only a partial solution, as high water levels are already damaging the foundations of the fragile palazzi. The British Venice in Peril Fund, committed to restoration of art and architecture and investigation into ways of protecting them, supports the project, whilst admitting that it doesn't address the chronic issue of rising water levels and the degradation of the lagoon, exacerbated by the digging

Venice in the rain

St Mark's mosaic

of deep navigation channels.

A further threat to the erosion of the city's foundations is the wash from boats on its waterways. To restrict the number of travellers and minimise further decay, vaporetto ticket prices for tourists have escalated in recent years.

The hot topic of mega-cruisers hugging the Venetian shores almost came to an end in 2014, with a short-lived ban on cruisers over 96,000 tonnes (the ban was lifted so a final decision is still pending at time of writing). A limit on smaller cruise ships is already in force.

DON'T LEAVE VENICE WITHOUT...

Taking a slow journey down the Grand Canal. Vaporetto No 1 chugs along Venice's famous waterway, giving you time to absorb the glorious parade of palaces. See page 36.

Popping into a backstreet *bacaro*. Join the locals for an *ombra* (glass of wine) and some sensational *cicchetti* (Venetian snacks) at one of the city's many *bacari*, traditional neighbourhood bars. The best ones tend to be around the Rialto. See page 70.

Lion-spotting. You'll see the leonine symbol of Venice all around the city. Pacific, playful or warlike, lions pose on flags unfurled over Grand Canal palaces, curl up in mosaics, fly as ensigns above ships, or crouch as statues in secret gardens. See how many you can spot.

Splashing out on a gondola. You may feel the total tourist, but taking a gondola is a once-in-a-life time experience. For romance, keep to the back canals rather than the Grand Canal. See page 132.

Taking in Venetian art. Churches and *scuole* (lay confraternities) are repositories of glowing treasures from the Venetian school. For the very best under one roof, head to the Accademia gallery in Dorsoduro. See page 42.

Exploring the Rialto. Join the Venetians at the morning markets, weave your way through a maze of back alleys, then brave the crowds on the bridge for a bird's-eye view of the Grand Canal. See page 70.

Visiting a Venetian mask-maker. Avoid the myriad fake masks and head for a traditional made-to-measure mask shop, where they can whip up anything from a festive Harlequin to a Medusa wreathed in snakes. See page 18.

Admiring the splendours of San Marco. Brave the crowds in Piazza San Marco, marvel at Basilica San Marco, the Doge's Palace and the sublime views across the lagoon. See page 28.

Stretching your legs along the Zattere. This broad sunny promenade along Dorsoduro's southern shore is flanked by cafés, churches, boathouses and galleries. At its tip the Punta della Dogana has been transformed into a cutting-edge contemporary art gallery. See page 57.

Taking a break at the Lido. Leave the bustle of the city behind, catch a vaporetto and chill out on the sandy beaches of Italy's first Lido. See page 85.

Pretty backstreet

Just as crucially, Venice may be mired in its glorious past, with Gothic palaces galore, but it needs to retain its population if it is to stave off its fate as a theme park. Venice's resident population, which was 200,000 in its heyday, has shrunk to 58,000, leaving the Venetians an endangered species. In a challenge to the city authorities, a pharmacy by the Rialto Bridge displays a monitor showing the (regularly updated) falling resident figures. Not only do visitors far outnumber locals, but the resident ageing population is being pushed out by rocketing rents and house prices, and all the extra costs that living in a lagoon city entails.

THE VENETIANS

Venetian residents are struggling to survive in a city dedicated to other people's dreams. But they are fighting back, carving out a space for themselves. Designer and activist Michela Scibilla and her 40 x Venezia pressure group are challenging the city to stop selling off its heritage. On Giudecca, gondola-maker 'Crea' continues to craft gondolas but is helping to save the boatyard by creating a new crafts centre – for ancient crafts.

All this despite the fact that the character of the city 'is old, conservative and resistant to change. Here in the historic centre we lack the capacity for renewal, or even the numbers required to effect a change', says Massimo Cacciari, the former mayor of Venice, speaking as ponderously and lugubriously as ever.

Yet the elusive Venetian spirit transcends such truisms, defies the simple arithmetic of the doom-mongers, and refuses to be confined by the straitjacket of tourism. Cool, independent Venetians are nothing if not survivors.

Cacciari is sanguine about the future: 'If Venice has any vitality left, it will seize the moment. If it is dead in human terms, it will die. After all, Babylon, Alexandria and Rome have all died.' While

Authentic Venice

Don't day-dream your way through the city but drift awhile with ordinary Venetians, and support sustainable tourism. Whether it's staying in a B&B, attending a Baroque recital, consuming sustainably sourced local food or doing a Venetian rowing course, you are helping Venice survive, with all its crafts and ancient skills, and getting to know Venetians at the same time. Before buying that cheap Taiwanese mask, call into a real craft shop and feel the difference. Rent a rococo costume from Atelier Nicolao (www.nicolao. com). Pick up some lion-encrusted stationery at Gianni Basso (see page 19). Glide into the lagoon and be a gondolier for a day with Row Venice. Book a ceramics workshop through the Venetian Club. Or chat to bookbinder Paolo Olbi (http://olbi.atspace.com) and caress the hand-tooled notebooks that caught Johnny Depp's attention.

A familiar sight   *Glass–blower in Murano*

at odds with the Venetians' positive approach to life, this view echoes their classic philosophical detachment. As such, the ex-mayor shows himself to be a contradictory character, and that is the mark of a true Venetian.

TOP TIPS FOR VISITING VENICE

Water, water everywhere. Venice has a higher average annual rainfall than London. Take an umbrella and, in autumn and winter, be prepared for *acqua alta* (high tide), when duckboards are laid out on low-lying piazzas and pavements.

Skip the queues. Book online at the main museums to avoid the crowds, or if you intend visiting several museums consider purchasing a Museumcard, either for the Museums of St Mark's Square or for the Palazzo Ducale and 10 other museums (www.vivaticket.it). The Venice Card (www.unicavenezia.it) covers museums and transport.

The price of people-watching. At any bar/café you pay a premium for waiter service. Grab an espresso from the bar for around a euro, but expect to pay up to €6 (Piazza San Marco price at time of writing) to sit and watch the world go by.

Reserve a table. As the best eateries are often both cramped and coveted by Venetians, call at least a day in advance to assure yourself a table. At weekends this is essential.

For a bird's-eye view. Two of the best vantage points in Venice are the campanile (bell tower) of San Giorgio Maggiore and the Skyline Rooftop Bar at the Hilton Molino Stucky on Giudecca, where you can enjoy sweeping views of Venice over cocktails.

Expect to get lost. Venice is a labyrinthine city, and losing your way is part of the fun of exploring. You are never very far from the yellow signs pointing to San Marco, Rialto and other key landmarks.

Crossing the Grand Canal. Save on a €7 single vaporetto (ferry) fare and cross the Grand Canal on a *traghetto* for €2. These gondolas ferry passengers across at seven points along the waterway. Venetians normally stand, but feel free to sit.

Ears to the ground. Keep your ears open for concerts as you stroll around and your eyes open for posters and flyers advertising them. For forthcoming performances and booking online, check out HelloVenezia (www.hellovenezia.com).

Fizz by the glass. If you fancy some bubbles but don't want to splash out on a whole bottle, ask for a glass *(un bicchiere)* of Prosecco. It is made in the Veneto and sold in every bar, usually fairly cheaply. The classic Venetian cocktail is a Bellini, Prosecco with peach juice.

Visiting for free. There is no charge for the Basilica of San Marco, the Salute church, the Rialto Markets, the Ghetto or the glass-blowing workshops on Murano. Watch out for free concerts in churches, open-air summer jazz events and (some) free events in February's Carnival.

Romantic al fresco dining

FOOD AND DRINK

The best places to head for when you're hungry in Venice are the authentic bars and everyday inns, known as bacari. This is where local people graze, in both new–wave and traditional bars, and usually with a Prosecco or spritz to hand.

Food critics tend to damn Venetian food as overpriced and underachieving, but you can eat well if you choose wisely. Even so, the difficulty of transporting fresh produce generally adds considerably to restaurant prices. Yet for seafood lovers, the cuisine can be memorable, with soft-shelled lagoon crabs, plump red mullet and pasta with lobster or black and pungent with cuttlefish ink.

VENETIAN CUISINE

According to top British chef and Italophile Alastair Little, 'The city's cosmopolitan past and superb produce imported from the Veneto have given rise to Italy's most eclectic and subtle style of cookery.' Like the Sicilians, the Venetians absorbed culinary ideas from the Arabs; they also raided Byzantium and, according to the Middle Eastern cookery writer Claudia Roden, translated it into their own simple style: 'If you could see the fish come in live at dawn in barges on the Grand Canal straight onto the market stalls, you would understand why all they want to do is lightly fry, poach or grill it.'

Culinary melting pot

As the hub of a cosmopolitan trading empire, Venice was bristling with foreign communities – Arabs, Armenians, Greeks, Jews and Turks – each with its own distinctive culinary tradition. Venetian trading posts in the Levant gave the city access to spices, the secret of subtle Venetian cookery. Pimiento, turmeric, ginger, cinnamon, cumin, cloves, nutmeg, saffron and vanilla show the oriental influences; pine nuts, raisins, almonds and pistachios also play their part. Drogheria Mascari (on Ruga degli Spezieri) remains the last of the scented spice shops that once dotted the Rialto.

Reflecting later conquests of Venice, these exotic ingredients are enriched with a dash of French or Austrian cuisine. From the end of the 18th century, French influence meant that oriental spices were supplanted by Mediterranean herbs.

The French brioche was added to the breakfast repertoire, as was the Turkish *crescente* (literally a crescent). The appearance of the croissant dates back to the Turkish defeat at the walls of Vienna in 1683. The Austrian conquest may have left Venice with a bitter taste

in its mouth, but it also left the city with a keen appetite for the conquerors' apple strudel and *krapfen* (doughnuts).

Eclectic tastes

A classic Middle Eastern-inspired dish is *sarde in saor*, tart sardines marinated in standard Venetian sauce. *Melanzane in saor*, made with aubergines, is the vegetarian version. *Saor* means savoury or tasty, and is a spicy sauce made with permutations of onions, raisins, vinegar, pine nuts and olive oil. *Riso* (rice), rather than pasta, predominates, prized for its versatility ever since its introduction by the Arabs. Creamy Venetian risotto offers endless possibilities, flavoured with spring vegetables, meat, game or fish. *Risi e bisi* (rice and peas) is a thick soup blended with ham, celery and onion. Equally delicious are the seasonal risottos, cooked with asparagus tips, artichoke hearts, fennel, courgettes or pumpkins. An oriental variant involves sultanas and pine nuts.

Fish dishes

Most local menus come from the Adriatic, but inland fishing also occurs in *valli*, fish farms in the lagoon, mainly for grey mullet *(cefalu)* and eel *(anguilla)*. It is hard to better *antipasti di frutti di mare*, a feast of simply cooked shellfish and molluscs, dressed with olive oil and lemon juice; prawns and soft-shelled crabs vie with baby octopus and squid. A trademark dish is cuttlefish risotto, served black and pungent with ink, or *granse-*

ola, spider crab, boiled and then dressed simply in lemon and oil. Another staple is *baccalà*, dried salt cod, prepared with milk and herbs or parmesan and parsley, and served in countless ways on *crostini*.

In Venice, fish predominates, but offal is also favoured, particularly in *fegato alla veneziana*, calves' liver sliced into ribbons and cooked with parsley and onions. It is always worth asking what specials (piatti del giorno) are on offer. These are often the freshest and most creative dishes on offer.

DESSERTS

Save room for pudding, because Venetian biscuits, cakes and desserts can be excellent, flavoured with exotic spices ever since the discovery of cinnamon and nutmeg. The Venetians introduced cane sugar to Europe, and have retained their sweet tooth. Spicy sweets are popular, including *fritelle di zucca*, sweet pumpkin doughnut served hot. Tiramisù is ubiquitous and varies widely. The best ices can be found in *gelaterie* such as Grom on Campo San Barnaba, or Nico on the Zattere.

TABLE TIPS

Beyond St Mark's, a number of individualistic restaurants have opened, and late-night dining has become more widespread. Weekly closing days vary, but are often Monday or Sunday. Reservations at restaurants are essential,

Fresh scallops at the Rialto market

especially at weekends. Also, remember most restaurants close between lunch and dinner, so if you are hungry between these times, pop into a bar for some *tramezzini* (little triangular sandwiches on white bread).

WHERE TO EAT

Venetian celebrity chef Enrica Rocca praises her home cuisine but also advises visitors to splash out on somewhere exceptional such as Ristorante Quadri, a current favourite: 'My philosophy of life is to eat one great meal and live on *cicchetti* for the rest of the time,' she teases. San Marco and Castello are home to some of the city's most prestigious restaurants, but privacy is rare in these goldfish-bowl settings. Further away from St Mark's, dining experiences tend to be more authentic, and more affordable. Try Cannaregio and the Rialto area for decent, well-priced meals. Not that visitors should ignore overtly glamorous spots; the Venetians patronise them too, including Caffè Quadri and Harry's Bar.

Styles of restaurant

Until recently, Venetian restaurants opted for cool, 18th-century elegance, or the exposed beams and copper pots that spell rustic gentility. Yet individualistic, even contemporary, inns now abound, whether tucked under pergolas or spilling onto terraces and courtyards. Reservations are required for the grander restaurants, which tend to be fairly dressy affairs, especially in the more elegant hotels. The opposite is true of the *bacari*, the traditional wine bars, where you could dress as a fishmonger if you felt like it.

More up-market places are termed *ristoranti*, but may be called *osterie* (inns) if they focus on homely food in an intimate or rustic setting. To confuse the issue, some inns have bars that act like traditional *bacari*, offering a full sit-down meal at a table, or quicker, cheaper nibbles at the bar. Even so, the distinction between bars and restaurants is somewhat blurred, as most *bacari* also serve food, typically the Venetian equivalent of tapas, known as *cicchetti*. Bars will offer a selection on their counters, typically polpette (spicy meatballs), carciofini (artichoke hearts), crostini with grilled vegetables, seppie rose (grilled cuttlefish) and anchovy nibbles. Keep track of what you eat as you'll be charged per piece (prices start from around €2). To eat *cicchetti e l'ombra*, a snack and a glass of wine, is a Venetian tradition.

DRINKS

Wine

The Veneto produces a number of superior (DOC) wines, from the fruity, garnet-red Bardolino to the less prestigious Valpolicella. Venetians drink far more white wine than red, partly through habit, partly because it is a better accompaniment to seafood.

Baccalà, a Venetian staple

Tempting pastries in Burano

Soave, which comes from vineyards dotted along the eastern shores of Lake Garda, can be rather bland. Dry whites from the Veneto and Friuli go particularly well with seafood dishes, as does the first vintage of Venetian wine from Venissa (see page 117), a vineyard that has recently been reclaimed from the lagoon.

Bacari are traditional wine bars and a traditional *giro di ombra* (bar crawl), especially in the authentic Rialto or Cannaregio areas, represents one of the highlights of any stay in Venice. The time-warp taverns are the perfect introduction to *cicchetti*.

Cocktails

Venice is noted for its cocktails, especially the Bellini, a peach-and-prosecco *aperitivo* created in the 1930s in Harry's Bar (see page 108). Prosecco, the sparkling wine from the Veneto, makes a fine aperitif, whether drunk dry *(secco)* or medium sweet *(amabile)*. It is drunk at the drop of a hat but is still distinctive enough for you to recognise a good one after a few days in Venice.

But to really look like a Venetian, risk the lurid orange cocktail known as a spritz (pronounced 'spriss' in Venetian dialect). The bright orange drink was introduced under Austrian rule (named after the introduction of 'selzer', fizzy soda water) and soon became a firm favourite. It consists of roughly equal parts of dry white wine, soda water and a herb-based aperitif, usually Campari,

Cynar or Aperol, and garnished with a twist of lemon or an olive. Ask for a *spritz al bitter* for a stronger, less cloying taste. The spritz may be an acquired taste, but once acquired, it's the clearest sign that you've fallen for Venice.

Where to drink

Not much changes in the historic cafés close to San Marco, where coffee has been drunk for centuries and post-prandial grappas downed since the days of the doges. Yet just beyond San Marco are serious wine bars *(enoteche)*, where tastings are the main draw. Over the last few years, there has been a trend for new wine bars, too, including cool reinterpretations of the *bacaro*; a few, such as Caffè Centrale, are sleek designer gastro-bars that would be at home in Manhattan – apart from the gondola moored by the back door. Even a number of once-staid hotel cocktail bars have been relaunched as cool lounge bars. As a result, Venetian bar culture is far broader than piano bars in sophisticated hotels.

Food and Drink Prices

Throughout this guide, we have used the following price ranges to indicate the approximate cost of a two-course meal for one with a glass of house wine:
€€€€ = over €85
€€€ = €55–85
€€ = €30–55
€ = up to €30

Masks for sale

SHOPPING

For sustainable shopping, seek out traditional Venetian crafts, from leather-bound notebooks to ceramics, luxury fabrics and marbled paper – but buy Murano glassware and masks only where the provenance is guaranteed.

To enjoy the excitement of finding something truly Venetian, you need curiosity, conviction and a sense of adventure. Craft shopping is an intimate experience, a secret glimpse of Venetians at their best. And, if the costs are quite high, remember that by supporting these ancient crafts, you are also supporting the city itself.

Most shops open Monday–Saturday from 9.30/10am until 12.30/1pm, then 3.30/4pm till 7.30/8pm. An increasing number also open on Sunday. Small shops may close on Monday morning. Some stores close either in August for the summer holiday or in January.

MASKS AND COSTUMES

If you want to buy a Venetian mask, always check what it is made of and ask the seller to tell you how it fits into the Venetian tradition – whether it is a character from the *commedia dell'arte* (see page 21), for instance. Just off Campo Santa Maria Formosa, Papier Mâché is an authentic mask shop (Calle Lunga S. Maria Formosa; www.papiermache.it). Here, over 30 years ago, Stefano Gottardo helped relaunch

Carnival and the moribund craft of mask-decorating. Since then, his distinctive one-off pieces have been sought after as design objects and featured in Stanley Kubrick's orgiastic *Eyes Wide Shut*. Mondonovo is one of the most creative mask-makers (Rio Terrà Canal, off Campo Santa Margherita, Dorsoduro 3063). Nearby, Ca' Macana (Calle della Botteghe, www.camacana.com) stocks traditional masks and offers mask-making courses.

TEXTILES

Venice is well known for Fortuny fabrics – silks and velvets, whether plain or gloriously patterned. Venetia Studium (Calle Larga XXII Marzo, San Marco 2403; www.venetiastudium.com) produces exclusive fabrics, including Fortuny designs, from scarves to cushion covers to lamps, as well as soft furnishings. Another big name in fabrics is Bevilacqua (Ponte della Canonica, San Marco 337b; also at San Marco 2520), which has been producing velvets and brocades since 1875; many are still produced on traditional 18th-century wooden looms.

Murano glassware

Jesurum (Fondamenta della Sensa, Cannaregio 3219) has been selling princely household linen, including embroidered sheets, since 1870. Frette (Calle Larga XXII Marzo, San Marco 2070a) sells fine linens, exquisite sheets, cushions and bathrobes. For finely made reproductions of historical costumes (as well as contemporary ones and accessories), made by the inmates of Giudecca's women's prison, head for Banco Lotto 10, Salizada Sant'Antonin, Castello 3478B.

MARBLED PAPER, BOOKS AND PRINTS

Between San Marco and the Rialto are shops selling marbled paper. Called *legatoria* or 'bookbinding', this ancient craft gives paper a decorative marbled veneer and is used nowadays for photograph albums, writing cases, greeting cards, diaries and notebooks. Good stockists include Cartavenezia (Calle Longa, Santa Croce 2125) and Paoli Olbi (Campo Santa Maria Nova, Cannaregio 6061), whose shop is stuffed with leather-bound notebooks studded with Venetian motifs, such as the Lion of St Mark. For prints, La Stamperia del Ghetto (Calle del Ghetto Vecchio, Cannaregio 1185a) includes general and Jewish themes. Gianni Basso (Calle del Fumo, Cannaregio 5306) churns out business cards, bookplates and stationery for clients all over the world in his tiny printing studio.

MURANO GLASS

It may be fashionable to mock Murano glass, but the best pieces are works of art, from show-stopping chandeliers to sophisticated sculpture signed by great Italian artists and designers. As the superior glassmakers mostly have showrooms clustered around San Marco, you could easily get a feel for the glassware on Murano, and see how it's made, before buying in Venice itself (prices are the same). Among the most prestigious contemporary glassmakers are Venini (shop on Piazzetta Leoncini, San Marco 314; factory and showrooms on Fondamenta Vetrai 50, Murano), and Barovier e Toso (Fondamenta Vetrai 28, Murano). In the Dorsoduro district, Napé Gallery sells collectors' pieces designed by virtuoso glassmakers, as well as quirky, everyday drinking glasses known as *goti* (http://www.murano900.com).

DESIGNER GOODS

Venice abounds in designer booty, but prices tend to be higher than on the mainland. The most elegant boutiques are to be found on Calle Vallaresso, Salizzada San Moisè, the Frezzeria as well as Calle Larga XXII Marzo, west of San Marco. But far more fun is the classic fabric and haberdashery quarter known as the Mercerie, a maze of alleys that winds between San Marco and the Rialto.

Masked revellers strike a pose

CARNIVAL

Venice Carnival is supreme self-indulgence, a giddy round of masked balls, parading along the waterfront, and private parties promising romance – a 'farewell to the flesh' that captivates the city in the run up to Shrove Tuesday

In some circles, it is fashionable to mock the carnival as a commercial fabrication, but its roots extend deep into the Venetian psyche. The people of this magnificent city on the lagoon have long had an instinctive love of spectacle and dressing up, dating back to the glory days of the Republic.

CARNIVAL HISTORY

Carnival reaches back to medieval times and represents a cavalcade of Venetian history, tracing political and military events, factional rivalries and defeats. The Venetian carnival is also the inheritor of a rich folk tradition, linked to the winter solstice. According to pagan rites, winter was a force to be overcome, with the sun persuaded to return by a show of life at its most vital.

Christianity afforded the carnival new significance: *carne vale*, from the Latin for 'farewell to meat', meant a last gasp, particularly on Mardi Gras (Fat Tuesday), before the start of the rigorous Lenten period, marked by abstinence from the pleasures of the flesh. In the past, the Venetian carnival was something of a movable feast, beginning as early as October or at Christmas time and lasting until Lent. In addition to masquerades, there were rope dancers, acrobats and fire-eaters, who routinely displayed their impressive skills on the Piazza San Marco.

The 17th-century English diarist John Evelyn (1620–1706) visited Venice in 1645–6 and reported on 'the folly and madness of the carnival', from the bull-baiting and the flinging of eggs to the superb opera, the singing eunuch and a shooting incident with an enraged nobleman and his courtesan, whose gondola canoodling he had disturbed.

During the 1751 carnival, everyone gathered to admire an exotic beast, the rhinoceros, captured in the famous painting Clara the Rhinoceros (1751) by the 18th-century Venetian artist Pietro Longhi and now displayed in the Ca' Rezzonico (see page 39).

When Napoleon conquered Venice in 1797, the carnival unfortunately went the tragic way of the Venetian Republic. Although it was revived sporadically in the early part of the 20th century, it was only fully restored in 1979. At that time, the event was eagerly reclaimed

A lady masquerader

by Venetians, with playful processions and masquerades.

CARNIVAL CAPERS

Thousands of masqueraders see in the carnival every year on Piazza San Marco. This event is followed by pantomime, operetta, parading and concerts in the city's *campi*.

In an attempt to reclaim carnival, however, Venetians are shifting celebrations to the neighbourhoods, including, for the first time in 2014, the Arsenale, but the set-pieces and the crowds still congregate on St Mark's Square.

The high point of the festival is Shrove Tuesday, when revellers gather for a masked ball on Piazza San Marco before moving on to private parties, notably Il Ballo del Doge (www.ilballodeldoge.com) the Doge's Ball. The end is signalled when the effigy of Carnival is burnt on Piazza San Marco.

CARNIVAL TODAY

Carnival has much to answer for: prices soar, and the city has more mask shops than butchers; fashion shoots and film crews swamp San Marco; cavorting crowds of motley Europeans dress as gondoliers, Casanovas and buxom courtesans. Yet despite the crowds and commercialism, this kitsch masquerade retains its magic.

Certainly, the Venetian love of disguise masks a desire to slip into a different skin. As Oscar Wilde said, 'A man only reveals himself when wearing a mask.' A mask also makes everyone equal. Masqueraders are addressed as '*sior maschera*' (masked gentleman) regardless of age, rank or even gender.

The most traditional masks are made of leather *(in cuoio)* or papier mâché *(in cartapesta)*, with modern creations worked in ceramics or covered with luxurious fabrics. To don a stunning disguise, visit the authentic Atelier Nicolao (www.nicolao.com). Choose a cloak and handcrafted mask or hire a full costume and slip back into the era of Casanova.

Commedia dell'Arte

A large number of the most distinctive carnival masks and costumes are inspired by characters from the *commedia dell'arte*. The essentially comic genre emerged in 16th-century Italy and featured improvisation, a fast pace and witty regional parodies. The plot was often secondary to the acrobatics, juggling and miming that kept the performance lively.

Stock characters based on regional stereotypes appeared in each performance, identified by their mask. Some of the most recognisable characters are: Arlecchino (Harlequin), the witty, clown-like servant from Bergamo; Pantalone, the miserly Venetian merchant; Dottore, the pompous scholar from Bologna; and Colombina, the wily and clever Venetian female counterpart to Arlecchino.

Classical concert in I Frari

ENTERTAINMENT

Outside the film festival, evening entertainment mostly takes the form of concerts and opera at La Fenice, a jewel of an opera house. Here we give the low-down on concerts, opera, music festivals and film.

CLASSICAL MUSIC

Venetians are passionate about their classical music and proud of the fact that Vivaldi, Monteverdi and Wagner all lived in the city. It helps that concerts are often held in beautiful settings, such as churches, oratories, frescoed palaces and the *scuole* (charitable confraternity seats). What's more, Venice is spearheading Italy's Baroque music revival, with musicians playing on authentic period instruments.

Autumn spells the start of the classical music season, and the start of the opera season at the reopened La Fenice (Campo San Fantin, San Marco; www.teatrolafenice.it; see page 46). Performances also take place in the diminutive Teatro Malibran (www.teatro lafenice.it), with ballet and concerts sometimes staged in Teatro Goldoni (www.teatrostabileveneto.it).

Confraternity concerts

The Scuola Grande di San Teodoro (tel: 041-521 0294; www.imusiciveneziani. it) stages concerts with singers and musicians dressed in 18th-century costumes. Concerts are also held in the sumptuous confraternity houses of the Scuola Grande di San Rocco (see page 65), the Scuola Grande dei Carmini, the Scuola Grande di San Giovanni Evangelista and the Ospedaletto.

Church concerts

One of the most popular concert churches is La Pietà (Riva degli Schiavoni), a rococo church linked to Vivaldi. It is a magnificent setting for the Venetian composer's work and for concerts of Baroque music in general.

If you ever dismissed Vivaldi as muzak, thanks to its misuse in so many commercial situations, do listen to the Interpreti Veneziani (www.interpretiveneziani.com) performing in the deconsecrated Chiesa San Vidal.

Classical concerts are also held in the Gothic church of I Frari (see page 66), in Tintoretto's church of Madonna dell'Orto (see page 76) and in La Salute (see page 58). The Renaissance church of Santa Maria dei Miracoli (see page 78), the Rialto market church of San Giacometto (www. ensembleantoniovivaldi.com) and the neighbourhood Santa Maria Formosa (see page 52) are also evocative set-

Opera performance in a Venetian palace

tings for concerts. On Piazza San Marco, the Ateneo di San Basso (www.virtuosodivenezia.com) is the setting for concerts of works by Vivaldi and Mozart.

Concerts in palaces

Concerts are also staged in the city's greatest palaces, from Ca' Vendramin-Calergi (where the music is usually Wagner) to Ca' Rezzonico, under a Tiepolo ceiling, no less (generally 18th-century music; see page 39).

Another extraordinary venue is the Collegium Ducale (Palazzo delle Prigioni, Castello; www.collegiumducale.it). Linked to the Doge's Palace by the Bridge of Sighs, these former prisons make a superb spot for opera and Baroque concerts. Palazzo Barbarigo-Minotto (Fondamenta Barbarigo o Duodo 2504, www.musicapalazzo.com) is a magical experience, with arias from Verdi and Rossini performed in a series of palatial salons. The frescoed Palazzetto Bru Zane (www.bru-zane.com), now restored to its former glory, is dedicated to French romantic music.

Open-air performances

In summer, key squares in the Dorsoduro district are turned into open-air concert venues, including Campo Pisani, just off Campo Santo Stefano. The 1,500-seat Teatro Verde (www.cini.it) on the island of San Giorgio Maggiore also makes a great setting for operatic performances. In September, the Venezia Suona festival is a long weekend of concerts taking place in squares and on abandoned islands.

LISTINGS AND BOOKINGS

For forthcoming concerts, check: www.musicinvenice.com. For opera, classical music and big-name concerts, book through HelloVenezia (www.hellovenezia.com; tel: 041-24 24); for indoor and outdoor jazz events and the Venice Jazz Festival (in July) visit www.venetojazz.com. For events generally it is also worth consulting the Venice tourist board website: www.turismovenezia.it.

Venice Film Festival

Although it does not have an indigenous film industry, Venice is the home of the world's oldest film festival, founded by Mussolini in 1932. For 10 days in September Venice plays host to Hollywood and European stars, plus the attendant paparazzi from all over the world. The festival is centred on the Lido, in the revamped Palazzo del Cinemà, built in 1930s Fascistic style. To spot the celebrities, stroll along the beach-side boulevard or splash out on a cocktail on the sea-view terrace of the Hotel Excelsior. The Bauer, Palazzina Grassi and Cipriani hotels are other favourite places to stay for the Hollywood set. During the festival, films are shown in their original versions. For more details, see www.labiennale.org/en/cinema.

La Fenice after the fire in 1996

HISTORY: KEY DATES

From its foundation among stagnant marshes on the shores of the Adriatic to glory days as the most powerful city in the West, Venice has seen it all. Thereafter came occupation and flooding, and now the tourists invade.

FIRST SETTLEMENTS

421	Foundation of Venice on 25 March, Feast Day of St Mark.
452–568	Attila the Hun plunders the Veneto. Mass migrations take place from the mainland to Venice.
697	The first doge, Paolo Lucio Anafesto, is elected to office.
814	The population moves to the more easily defended Rivo Alto (Rialto). Venetian coins first minted. Work begins on the first Doge's Palace.

HEIGHT OF THE REPUBLIC

828	St Mark's body is taken from Alexandria to Venice.
1000	Venice controls the Adriatic coast.
1095–9	Venice joins the Crusades, providing ships and supplies for First Crusade to liberate the Holy Land.
1173	First Rialto Bridge begun.
1202–4	Fourth Crusade; the sack of Constantinople and Venetian conquest of Byzantium provide a springboard for the growth of the Venetian empire. Arsenale shipyards are created. Venice becomes a world power.
1309–10	Work begins on the present Doge's Palace. The Council of Ten is set up as a check on individual power and a security monitor.
1348–9	A plague outbreak kills half the people of Venice.
1453–4	Constantinople falls to the Turks; zenith of Venetian empire: Treviso, Bergamo, Ravenna, Friuli, Udine and Istria are all conquered.
1489	Cyprus is ceded to Venice by Queen Caterina Cornaro.
1508	League of Cambrai unites Europe against Venice. Titian's *Assumption* is hung in the Frari church.

Palazzo Ducale interior   *The frozen lagoon in 1708*

1571	Battle of Lepanto, a decisive naval victory against the Turks.
1577	Veneto-born Andrea Palladio designs Il Redentore church.
1669	Loss of Crete, the last major Venetian colony, to the Turks.
1708	A harsh winter freezes the lagoon; Venetians walk to the mainland.
1718	Venice surrenders Morea (Peloponnese) to the Turks, signalling the loss of its maritime empire.
1790	Opening of La Fenice opera house.

UNDER OCCUPATION

1797	Fall of the Republic. Napoleon grants Venice to Austria.
1800	Papal conclave in Venice to elect a pope.
1805–14	Napoleonic rule reinstated.
1815–66	Under the Congress of Vienna, Austria occupies the city.
1846	Venice is joined to the mainland by a railway causeway.
1861	Vittorio Emanuele is crowned king of a united Italy.
1866	Venice is annexed to the Kingdom of Italy.

20TH CENTURY TO THE PRESENT

1931	A road causeway connects city to mainland.
1945	British troops liberate the city from Nazi occupiers.
1960	Construction of the Marco Polo airport.
1966	The worst flood in Venetian history hits the city.
1979	The Venice Carnival is revived.
1988	First stage of MOSE (Moses) mobile flood barrier completed.
1996	Burning down of La Fenice opera house. The worst floods and *acqua alta* (high tides) since 1966.
2004	La Fenice reopens after reconstruction, with *La Traviata*.
2008	The controversial Ponte Calatrava is constructed across the Grand Canal, linking the railway station with Piazzale Roma.
2009	The Punta della Dogana is relaunched as a showcase for contemporary art from the collection of French magnate François Pinault.
2011	The Bridge of Sighs is restored to its former glory.
2013	The MOSE mobile barrier passes its first test.
2014	Santiago Calatrava faces legal action over alleged errors in the construction of his Grand Canal bridge.

BEST ROUTES

The domes of the Basilica San Marco

PIAZZA SAN MARCO

Piazza San Marco is the focus of Venetian life. Start with the splendours of the Basilica and the Doge's Palace, then saunter along the Riva degli Schiavoni, relax in a café and absorb the sublime views across the lagoon.

DISTANCE: 1km (0.6 miles)
TIME: A full day
START: Basilica San Marco
END: Torre dell' Orologio
POINTS TO NOTE: Booking a slot to visit the Basilica at www.venetoinside.com at least two days before your visit means that you won't have to queue. Another way to avoid queuing is to check in a bag (no large bags or backpacks are allowed inside) at the Ateneo S. Basso (Calle S. Basso, by the Piazzetta dei Leoncini). You will be given a tag that can be taken to the guards and will allow you to skip the queue. To get the best views of the mosaics, visit when the Basilica is illuminated, from 11.30am–12.30pm daily. To avoid the crowds, go early morning or late afternoon, avoiding weekends, if possible. Beware that visitors are usually herded through the Basilica and encouraged to spend no more than 10 minutes during a visit. Scantily dressed visitors, eg those wearing shorts or with uncovered shoulders, will be turned away.

Piazza San Marco, famously dubbed 'the most elegant drawing room in Europe' by Napoleon, is the focal point of Venice. It is the only square in the city important enough to be called a piazza. Before braving the hordes in the Basilica, consider splashing out on a coffee or Prosecco at **Florian**, see ❶, prince of the city's coffee houses and haunt of such literary giants as Byron, Dickens and Proust. Linger as long as you like, preferably alfresco, to admire one of the most often-praised squares in the world.

You may notice a conspicuous absence of the famed pigeon-feed vendors in the piazza. They were banned by the city in 2008, as it was proved that the pigeon droppings were causing damage to the monuments. Anyone now seen feeding pigeons in the square faces a fine.

ST MARK'S BASILICA

The centrepiece of the square is the sumptuous **Basilica San Marco** ❶ (Piazza San Marco; www.basilicasanmarco.it; Mon-Sat 9.45am–5pm, Sun 2–4pm; Pala d'Or and Treasury close

Gilded mosaics in the Basilica

at 4pm daily Nov–Easter; charge only for Museo di San Marco, Pala d'Oro and Treasury), the shrine of the Republic and symbol of Venetian glory. Before joining the queue for the Basilica, take a close look at the external sculpture, mosaics and the four horses above the central portal. These are replicas of the originals, which were looted from Constantinople during the Fourth Crusade. They were moved to the Museo di San Marco inside the Basilica to protect them from pollution.

Myriad mosaics

Of all the mosaics decorating the entrances and upper portals, the only original is *The Translation of the Body of the Saint* above the door on the far left. Look closely to see how the Basilica looked in the 13th century. The lower portal on the far right has a mosaic showing how the body of St Mark was taken from Alexandria, reputedly smuggled under slices of pork. Turbaned Muslims are showing their revulsion at the smell – the figure in the blue cloak is holding his nose.

The atrium mosaics are some of the finest in the Basilica: on the right **The Genesis Cupola** describes the *Creation of the World* in concentric circles, followed by scenes from the stories of Noah. Either side of the central portal are the oldest mosaics in the Basilica, *The Virgin with Apostles and Saints*.

Museo di San Marco

Take the steep narrow steps up to the **Museo di San Marco**, the gallery above

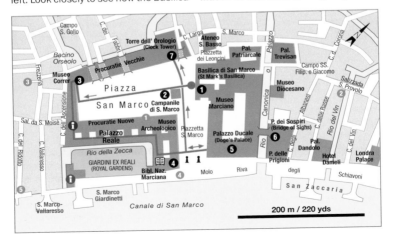

The Torre dell' Orologio also tells the sign of the zodiac

the entrance portal. Note that if you are planning to see all or most of the museums in the piazza, it is worth purchasing a cumulative ticket (www.visitmuve.it), for the San Marco Museums – the Palazzo Ducale, Museo Correr, Museo Archeologico Nazionale and Biblioteca Marciana – which was €16 at time of writing. It is certainly worth the admission fee to see the Basilica's original **bronze horses**, and, from the outside **Loggia dei Cavalli,** the grandstand view of the Piazza and Piazzetta, just as doges and dignitaries did during processions and celebrations.

As you look into the Basilica from the gallery, the interior appears cavernous. The mosaics cover some 4,000 sq m (43,000 sq ft) of floor, domes, arches and walls. The *pavimento* is like an oriental carpet, embellished with naturalistic and religious motifs, its undulations proving how movable the foundations of the church are.

Back at ground level, don't miss the first two domes in the nave for some of the finest of the mosaics: the **Pentecost Dome**, which shows the Descent of the Holy Ghost as a dove, and the Ascension Dome, featuring Christ in Glory surrounded by Apostles, angels and the Virgin Mary.

The altarpiece and other treasures

The greatest of many treasures is the **Pala d'Oro**, a superb medieval screen behind the altar. First commissioned for Doge Pietro Orseolo in the 9th century, and increasingly enriched over the years,

it is made up of 250 panels, encrusted with pearls, sapphires, emeralds and enamels. Even after Napoleon's looting, there are still about 2,000 jewels left.

More Byzantine loot is stored in the **Treasury** (entered from the right transept). The prize piece here is the Pyx, an embossed silver-gilt casket in the shape of a Byzantine church. There are many other beautiful features in the Basilica, among them the **Baptistery** and **Zen Chapel** (both usually closed to the public, but accessible on guided tours, www.venetoinside.com), the chapels and the rood screen.

THE CAMPANILE

The well-restored **Campanile ❷** (Bell Tower; daily July–Sept 9am–9pm, Apr–June and Oct 9am–7pm, Nov–Easter 9.30am–3.45pm; charge) looks much as it did when it assumed its present form in the early 16th century. This would not be surprising were it not for the fact that it collapsed in a heap on 14 July 1902. Amazingly, the only casualties were the custodian's cat and, at the foot of the tower, Sansovino's Loggetta, which was reassembled from the debris. The campanile was rebuilt exactly 'dov'era e com'era' ('where it was and how it was'). A lift takes you to the top for stunning views of the city and lagoon, and stretching on a clear day to the peaks of the Dolomites; oddly, the canals are not visible. During the Republic, each of the bells played a different role, with one summoning

Palazzo Ducale   *Winged lion on the Basilica facade*

senators to the Doge's Palace, another announcing a session of the Senate and the smallest, the execution bell, literally sounding the death knell.

ACQUA ALTA

The plaque by the exit of the Campanile marks the water level on 4 November 1966 – about 0.9m (3ft) above the pavement of Piazza San Marco, the lowest point of the city. This was the worst flood in Venetian history. Deadly flooding or *acqua alta* (high water) invades the piazza some 250 times a year. A controversial new tidal barrier named MOSE (after the prophet Moses, who parted the waves) has been built to protect the city should be fully in action by 2016. For now, whenever the square floods, duckboards are laid down so that people can cross without getting wet feet. It is a novelty for tourists, but a headache for the city authorities.

CORRER MUSEUM

Opposite the Basilica, on the Piazza's far side, the **Museo Correr ❸** (Piazza San Marco; www.correr.visitmuve.it; daily Apr–Oct 10am–6pm, Nov–Mar 10am–4pm; charge) occupies some 70 rooms of the Procuratie Nuove (Offices of the Former Procurators of St Mark's) and the Ala Napoleonica (Napoleonic Wing).

The museum is refreshingly free of crowds and full of historical and artistic treasures. Some grasp of Venetian history helps, though there are useful information sheets in English in each room. A new itinerary leads through the lavishly decorated Imperial Rooms of the Royal Palace, which opened in 2012 after 10 years of restoration.

The Elizabeth of Austria, known as Empress Sissi, resided here during her visits to Venice in 1856–7 and 1861–2 and the rooms include her boudoir, elegantly decorated with corn flowers and lilies of the valley – her favourite flowers.

The first floor is occupied by 20 rooms devoted to the life and culture of the Venetian Republic with sections on the institution of the doge, Venetian trade and the Arsenale. A highlight is the *Bucintoro*, the ship used to transport the doge during special processions (room 45).

Venetian art

Art-lovers should concentrate on the **Quadreria**, inconspicuously located in rather gloomy rooms on the second floor. A fine collection of Venetian Renaissance works includes a room of works by the Bellinis (room 36) and the famous Carpaccio painting *Two Venetian Noblewomen* (room 38), formerly called *The Courtesans*. The ladies look bored as they wait for their husbands to return from a hunting trip. Also worth seeking out is the detailed wood engraving of Venice carved by Jacopo de' Barbari in 1500 (room 32).

The museum also gives access, via rooms 18 and 19, to the **Museo**

The Piazzetta

Archeologico (Archaeology Museum), full of Greek and Roman statuary. A highlight is the 1st-century BC Grimani Altar (room 6), with Bacchic decoration and a sensual relief of lovers in an embrace.

MARCIANA LIBRARY

Also accessible from the Museo Correr is the **Biblioteca Marciana ❹** (Marciana Library, also known as the Libreria Sansoviana; www.marciana.venezia. sbn.it; daily Apr−Oct 9am−7pm, Nov−Mar 9am−5pm; charge), whose main hall (Sala Monumentale) has a magnificent ceiling with allegorical scenes painted by artists such as Tintoretto and Veronese.

The library building, which you can admire from the Piazzetta, was built by Sansovino in 1530 to house the doge's precious collection of Greek and Latin manuscripts. Palladio described it as 'the richest building since antiquity'. But the construction was not without problems. The vaulting collapsed, Sansovino was blamed and promptly imprisoned. He was released only after appeals from acquaintances in high places.

The architect was also responsible for the severe-looking **Zecca**, where Venice minted gold and silver ducats until the fall of the Republic. The mint and treasury functioned until 1870 but is now part of the Marciana Library, with the courtyard covered over and used as a reading room.

LUNCH BREAK

It is probably time for lunch and a rest from sightseeing. Everything around the Piazza is criminally overpriced. If you're happy to splurge, enjoy the stunning views from the rooftop terrace of the **Hotel Danieli** (see page 99); if you prefer an affordable trattoria patronised by Venetians, try **Alla Rivetta**, see ❷ behind the Riva degli Schiavoni or Osteria Da Carla, on the far side of Piazza San Marco, see ❸.

PALAZZO DUCALE

From the 9th century to the fall of the Republic in 1797, the **Palazzo Ducale ❺** (Doge's Palace; Piazza San Marco; www. palazzoducale.visitmuve.it; daily Apr−Oct 8.30am−7pm, Nov−Mar 8.30am−5.30pm; charge) was the powerhouse of Venice. It was the residence of the doges, seat of the government and venue of the law courts and prisons. By the 14th century the Venetian head of state was little more than a figurehead, or 'a glorified slave of the Republic', as Petrarch put it. But as far as living quarters went, the doge couldn't complain. No other residence could rival it, and for many years this was the only building in Venice entitled to the name *palazzo*. Other grand residences had to be satisfied with the appellation Ca', short for *casa* (house).

The ceremonial entrance, on the Piazzetta, was the **Porta della Carta**, a magnificent piece of flamboyant Gothic

Biblioteca Marciana exhibit

The Molo, as painted by Canaletto

architecture, showing Doge Foscari kneeling before the Lion of St Mark. Today this is the public exit, the entrance being the **Porta del Frumento** on the waterfront. From this side you can admire the shimmering pink facade, the delicate arches and the florid Gothic detail.

Palace interior

Located near the entrance, the **Museo dell'Opera** (Works Museum) houses some of the original richly carved capitals from the palace. From here you go into the main courtyard, whose **Scala dei Giganti** (Giants' Staircase) formerly made an appropriately grandiose entry to the palace.

Inside the palace the great chambers were the meeting place for the highest levels of political and administrative systems. Huge rooms are decorated with heavily encrusted ceilings and monumental canvases, all in glorification of the great Venetian Republic. Leading artists of the day, including Tintoretto and Veronese, were commissioned to convey the idea that Venice was not just a place of power, but also one of overwhelming beauty.

The sumptuous **Scala d'Oro** (Golden Staircase) leads up to the doge's private apartments, then up again to the grand Council Chambers. The most impressive among these are the **Anticollegio**, the waiting room for ambassadors, with Veronese's *Rape of Europe* and works by Tintoretto; the **Sala del Collegio**, with magnificent ceiling paintings by Veronese; and the **Sala del Senato**, with another elaborate ceiling, painted by Tintoretto and assistants. It was in the **Sala del Consiglio dei Dieci** that the notoriously powerful Council of 10 (in fact about 30) tried crimes against the state. Secret denunciations were posted in the *bocca di leone* (lion's mouth) in the waiting room.

After the armoury, you go back to the second floor, along Liagò Gallery, to the grandest room of all: the **Sala del Maggior Consiglio**. This was the Assembly Hall, where doges were elected and where the last doge abdicated. The proportions are monumental – some 3,000 guests were accommodated when Henry III of France was entertained here at a state banquet in 1574. The ceiling consists of panels painted by famous contemporary artists, among them Tintoretto and Veronese, whose dynamic *Apotheosis of Venice* stands out for its dramatic perspective. Tintoretto's huge *Paradise*, which covers the entire east wall, was for a long time the largest painting in the world: a staggering feat for a man of 70. Below the ceiling a frieze features the first 76 doges. Note the blacked-out space that should depict Marin Falier, the doge executed for treason in 1355.

Bridge of Sighs

From the splendour of the council rooms you are plunged, as were the prisoners, into the dungeons. The *pozzi*, the dun-

Caffè Florian

geons beneath the palace, were dark, dank and infested with rats; the *piombi*, where Casanova entertained and masterminded his daring escape, were salubrious in comparison. The new prisons, those you see today, are reached via the renovated **Ponte dei Sospiri** ⑥ (Bridge of Sighs) – named after the sighs of prisoners as they took a last look at freedom before torture or execution. Or so the story goes. In fact, by the time the bridge was built in the 17th century, the cells were quite civilised by European standards, and used only to house petty offenders. Only one political prisoner ever crossed the bridge.

The Secret Itinerary

The 'Secret Itinerary' is a fascinating tour, in English, French or Italian, of the hidden parts of the palace, such as the torture chamber and dungeons (tours in English daily Sept–June 9.55am, 10.45am and 11.35am; booking essential, tel: 041-240 7238, or at the Palazzo Ducale information desk).

THE PIAZZETTA

Bounded by the mint, the Basilica and the Doge's Palace is the Piazzetta (Little Square) overlooking the waterfront. The quayside known as Bacino San Marco, is where foreign dignitaries and ambassadors would moor their boats as they entered the city – now there is a lively gondola stand. Pop into **Al Todaro**, see ④, for a quick coffee among the gondo-

liers, and observe the enormous granite columns of **San Marco and San Teodoro**, brought from Constantinople in the 12th century. The engineer who miraculously managed to set up the columns in 1172 was rewarded with the gambling monopoly in Venice. Executions frequently took place between the pillars and superstitious Venetians never walk between the two.

One column is topped by a statue of St Theodore, who was the original patron saint of the city before St Mark's remains were brought to Venice from Alexandria. The other column is surmounted by what appears to be a winged lion, the traditional symbol for St Mark. It is now believed this lion is actually a chimera, brought back from China; the Venetians simply added wings and transformed it into the lion of St Mark.

TORRE DELL' OROLOGIO

To the west of Piazza San Marco is the **Bacino Orseolo**, the main gondola depot, is an ideal spot for watching water traffic. If you decide to hop on board don't pay more than the official rate (evening trips are extra), and agree a route before setting off. For romance, stick to the back canals rather than the Grand Canal.

The basin backs onto the **Procuratie Vecchie**, once the lavish apartments of Venice's nine procurators or top-ranking officials. At the far end of the building, over the archway, stands

Moored gondolas

The Bridge of Sighs

the Renaissance **Torre dell' Orologio** ❼ (Clock Tower; tel: 041-427 30892; www.torreorologio.visitmuve. it; guided tours in English Mon–Wed at 10am, 11am, Thur–Sun at 2pm and 3pm; reserve ahead; charge). It has a large gilt-and-blue enamel clock face, which displays the signs of the zodiac and phases of the moon. It also, of course, tells the time, with two bronze figures of Moors striking the bell on the hour. The clock draws large crowds at Ascension, when the figures of the Magi emerge from side doors to pay their respects to the Virgin and Child, set above the clock. Behind the Clock Tower, shoppers can plunge into the dark alleys of the **Mercerie**. Or flee the crowds to collapse in the waterfront café **L'Ombra del Leone**, see ❺.

Food and Drink

❶ CAFFÈ FLORIAN
Piazza San Marco; tel: 041-520 5641; Thur–Tue; €€
The renowned Florian is the place for a Prosecco or a Venetian spritz in style, while drowning in dubious musical offerings. You pay more when the band strikes up.

❷ ALLA RIVETTA
Castello 4625, Ponte San Provolo; tel: 041-528 7302; Tue–Sun; €€
Set by the bridge linking Campo Santi Filippo e Giacomo and Campo San Provolo, this is an unpretentious, un-touristy place close to San Marco. Fish, polenta and plates of roast vegetables predominate.

❸ OSTERIA DA CARLA
Corte Contarina, Frezzeria 1535a; tel: 041-523 7855; Mon-Sat; €
This ancient *osteria* is tucked away in a courtyard only 100m away from Piazza San Marco but feels a far cry from the bustle.

Venetians, including gondoliers, pop in for *cicchetti* (Venetian tapas) or tuck into authentic local dishes. Service can be a bit off-hand for non-locals, especially at busy times. Reserve a table or be prepared to queue.

❹ AL TODARO
Piazzetta San Marco 3; tel: 041-528 5165; daily, Tue–Sun in winter; €
A nice alternative to the formal, and more expensive, cafés on the Piazza, this one is frequented by gondoliers from the nearby stand. Does coffee and delicious ice creams. Outdoor seating only. Opens late.

❺ L'OMBRA DEL LEONE
Ca' Giustinian, Calle del Ridotto, San Marco 1364/A; tel. 041-241 2167; daily; €€
Set in the waterfront Biennale headquarters, this contemporary arty café overlooks St Mark's and La Salute. It's a peaceful spot for a coffee or Prosecco, with the terrace perfect for a light lunch. The menu changes daily but usually includes pasta and salads.

The Grand Canal from the controversial new Ponte della Costituzione

VAPORETTO DOWN THE GRAND CANAL

The Grand Canal sweeps majestically through the heart of the city, lined with palaces and teeming with traffic of all descriptions, from gondolas to garbage barges. You can see it all from a vaporetto (waterbus) on this tour.

DISTANCE: 4km (2.5 miles)
TIME: 40 mins on vaporetto No. 1 (30 mins on No. 2)
START: Piazzale Roma vaporetto landing stage
END: San Zaccaria vaporetto landing stage
POINTS TO NOTE: A single vaporetto ticket (lasting one hour) costs €7, so if you are intending to take other ferry trips during your stay, consider one of the ferry passes: €20 for 24 hours, €25 for 36 hours, €30 for 48 hours, €35 for 72 hours, €50 for a week. These can be pre-booked at www.hellovenezia.com or bought on arrival at Piazzale Roma, either at the Hello Venezia or ACTV office.

The Grand Canal, Venice's fabulous highway, is nearly 4km (2.5 miles) long. The surprisingly shallow waterway is spanned by four bridges and lined by 10 churches and more than 200 palaces. It sweeps through six city districts *(sestieri)*, providing changing vistas of palaces and warehouses, markets and merchant clubs, courts, prisons and even the city casino. You can see it all from vaporetto No. 1, the waterbus that takes it slowly, stopping at every landing stage; No. 2 makes the same journey, with only six stops.

The route starts from **Piazzale Roma** ❶, in the north of Venice. You could do it the other way round, starting from San Marco, but this way you have the grand finale of the Santa Maria della Salute church. You could start at the railway station (Stazione Ferroviaria), but you are guaranteed the best views from a seat at the open-air front of the boat; for this, you need to be one of the first to embark, at Piazzale Roma.

The canal has a speed limit of 7kmh (4mph), but motor boats and taxis rarely respect it. No craft apart from gondolas, or public or commercial transport, can go on the Grand Canal before 6pm.

TOWARDS THE STATION

As you ride towards the station, you'll have a good view of the **Ponte**

The Fondaco dei Turchi, Venice's Natural History Museum

della Costituzione – Venice's newest bridge, unveiled in 2008 and named to celebrate the 60th anniversary of the Italian Constitution. It was designed by acclaimed Spanish architect Santiago Calatrava (it is familiarly known as the Ponte Calatrava) and connects Piazzale Roma with the railway station. A minimalist structure of steel, glass and stone, the sinuous, fish-tailed bridge has courted huge controversy, especially for its lack of wheelchair access, errors in design and for its inexplicably huge maintenance costs. After a 5-year wait a moveable enclosed pod alongside the bridge is now finally in action for those with mobility problems.

Stazione Ferroviaria Santa Lucia ➋ comes into view on your left. This striking modern building was built in 1954, with its stairway offering visitors their first taste of the Venetian lagoon. By

the station, the Baroque church of the **Scalzi** was named after the 'barefooted' *(scalzi)* Carmelite friars who founded it in the 17th century. In 1915 an Austrian bomb hit the roof, which was decorated with a fresco by Tiepolo. Fragments of the work are now in the Accademia. The vaporetto passes under the **Ponte degli Scalzi**, built in 1934 to replace a 19th-century iron structure.

FONDACO DEI TURCHI TO THE PESCHERIA

Opposite the San Marcuola stop the **Fondaco dei Turchi ➌** was a stunning Veneto-Byzantine construction before it was heavily restored in the 19th century. The former warehouse was leased to Turkish merchants; today it is home to the Museum of Natural History (June–Oct daily 10am–6pm, Nov–May Tue–Fri 9am–5pm, Sat and Sun

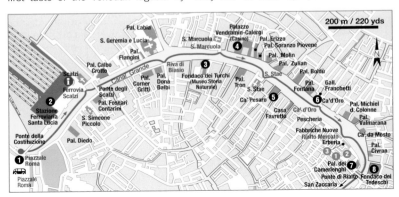

10am–6pm, www.msn.visitmuve.it), reopened after major restoration. Just past the landing stage on the left, the vast **Palazzo Vendramin-Calergi** ❹ is one of the canal's finest Renaissance palaces, designed by Mauro Coducci. Wagner died here in 1883. Today, it is home to the city's casino. To admire the palace from afar, leave the boat at San Stae or to gamble in the impressive casino (daily 3pm–2am, ID required), get off at San Marcuola.

Beyond the Baroque church of San Stae on your right looms the **Ca' Pesaro** ❺, designed by the Venetian Baroque architect, Baldassare Longhena. It houses the **Gallery of Modern Art and Oriental Art Museum** (both Tue–Sun 10am–6pm, 10am–5pm Nov–Mar; charge, www.capesaro.visitmuve.it). Beyond it the white Ca' Corner della Regina was the birthplace of Caterina Cornaro, queen of Cyprus, in 1454.

The vaporetto recrosses the canal to the **Ca' d'Oro** ❻ landing stage, by the palace of the same name. This is a landmark building, a sumptuous version of a Venetian palace. The pink-and-white filigree facade, with carved capitals, crowning pinnacles and bas-reliefs, was once covered in gold leaf – hence the name, House of Gold. The original owner, Marino Contarini, demolished a palace to construct this magnificent building in the early 15th century. The Gothic palace houses the **Galleria Franchetti**, one of the city's most appealing art galleries.

Pescheria and Erberia

The next vaporetto stop is Rialto Mercato, where fresh fish is laid out on ice under the colonnades of the mock-Gothic **Pescheria** (fish market; closed Mon); vegetables, fruit and flowers are sold at the adjoining Erberia. Barges from the island of Sant' Erasmo arrive early in the morning to offload crates of lagoon artichokes and asparagus. The Rialto Mercato vaporetto landing stage leads to both the bustling market and the café-lined waterfront, now one of the most sought-after spots for sunset cocktails and *cicchetti* or for embarking on a bar crawl.

If you have a pass and are able to hop on and off the vaporetto at your leisure, the Erberia holds many options for eating on the canal, see ❶, ❷ and ❸.

AROUND THE RIALTO

Gondolas and traffic congestion are likely to slow you down at the **Rialto**, giving you time to take in the bridge and surrounding buildings. Just before the bridge on the right the **Palazzo dei Camerlenghi** ❼ (1528) was formerly the office of the city treasurers (*camerlenghi*). Later, it served as the state prison. Opposite, the **Fondaco dei Tedeschi** ❽, named after the German merchants who leased the emporium, and conducted a healthy trade in precious metals from German mines, this was the most important trading centre in the Rialto area. Controversially sold to the Veneto-based clothing

retailer Benetton in 2008 for £45 million, this 500-year-old landmark building, for many years the main post office, has finally got the go-ahead for its controversial conversion into a shopping centre/cultural space by Dutch architect Rem Koolhaas.

RIALTO BRIDGE TO CA' FOSCARI

Next you pass the **Ponte di Rialto** (Rialto Bridge), constructed in 1588–91 after two of the previous wooden bridges had collapsed. Michelangelo, Palladio and Sansovino were among the eminent contenders for the commission for the new stone structure, but in the end the project went to the aptly named Antonio da Ponte.

Before the San Silvestro stop, on the left, are the arcaded palaces of **Ca' Loredan** and **Ca' Farsetti**, both now occupied by the mayor and city council. Beyond, the large, austere-looking **Palazzo Grimani** ❾ is a Renaissance masterpiece by Michele Sanmicheli, and now serves as the Court of Appeal.

Just before the Sant'Angelo stop, note the Renaissance **Palazzo Corner-Spinelli** ❿ (1490–1510), designed by Mauro Coducci and distinguished by its arched windows and rusticated ground floor. This became a prototype for many other *palazzi* in Venice.

Stopping at San Tomà gives you time to look across to **Palazzo Mocenigo** ⓫. Byron lived here for two years, renting the *palazzo* for £200 a year. His affair with his housekeeper ('of considerable beauty and energy... but wild as a witch and fierce as a demon') ended with the brandishing of knives and his lover hurling herself into the Grand Canal. Right on La Volta (the bend of the canal), recognisable by its distinctive pinnacles, **Palazzo Balbi** ⓬ was the chosen site for Napoleon to watch the regatta of 1807, held in his honour.

On the same side, across the tributary (Rio Foscari) the **Ca' Foscari** ⓭ was described by the art critic John Ruskin as 'the noblest example in Venice of 15th-century Gothic'. Now restored, the palace was built in 1437 for Doge Francesco Foscari; today it is the most prestigious university building.

CA' REZZONICO TO THE ACCADEMIA

The next stop is **Ca' Rezzonico** ⓮, named after what is arguably the finest Baroque palace in Venice. Designed in 1667 by Baldassare Longhena, it was at one time owned by Robert Browning's reprobate son, Pen. It was while Robert Browning was staying here that he died of bronchitis. Now the **Museo del Settecento Veneziano** (Museum of 18th-century Venice; Wed–Mon 10am–6pm, Nov–Mar 10am–5pm; charge), it has a suitably grandiose rococo interior, decorated with massive chandeliers, frescoed ceilings and lacquered furniture. The second floor is a gallery of 18th-century Venetian paintings, while the third is

Gilded gondola on the Grand Canal

home to the **Egidio Martini Picture Gallery**, an eclectic collection spanning five centuries. In terms of Venetian art, Ca' Rezzonico takes up where the Accademia (see page 42) leaves off.

Palazzo Grassi and the Accademia
Opposite Ca' Rezzonico is the **Palazzo Grassi** ⓖ, a fine example of an 18th-century patrician residence, bought in 2005 by the French business magnate François Pinault to house his huge collection of contemporary art.

The wooden **Ponte dell'Accademia** ⓖ (Accademia Bridge) was built as a temporary structure in the 1930s to replace a heavy iron bridge. The Venetians were so pleased with it, however, that it was retained. Beside the bridge on the right is the **Accademia** (see page 42).

PALAZZO BARBARO TO SAN ZACCARIA

Beyond the bridge, the second and third adjoining buildings on the left are the Gothic **Palazzi Barbaro** ⓖ. The second was a haunt of writers and artists, when the palace belonged to the Bostonian Curtis family. Among the guests were Robert Browning, John Singer Sargent, Monet, Whistler,

and Henry James who wrote *The Aspern Papers* here and used it as a setting for *The Wings of a Dove*.

Peggy Guggenheim Collection and Palazzo Dario
On the right, the 18th-century **Palazzo Venier dei Leoni** ⓖ, or Palazzo Nonfinito (Unfinished Palace), which houses the **Peggy Guggenheim Collection** (see page 59).

Two blocks on, the palace with the coloured marble and distinctive chimneys is the charming but reputedly cursed **Palazzo Ca' Dario** ⓖ, built for a Venetian diplomat. Over the centuries there has been a history of murder, bankruptcy and suicide here. The last victim

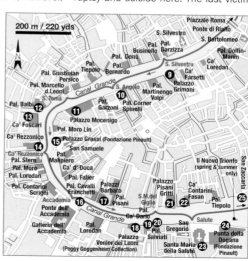

Palazzo Salviati   *Taxi boat near Ponte dell'Accademia*

was industrialist Raul Gardini, owner of the palace from 1985, who apparently shot himself during the corruption investigations of 1993.

Palazzo Salviati to Palazzo Pisani-Gritti

Just beyond Palazzo Dario, you'll note **Palazzo Salviati ⑳**, built in 1924 for a glass-blowing family. They took advantage of their prime real estate for a little self-advertisement: the prominent mosaic is wholly out of place with the Renaissance-style architecture.

Beyond the Santa Maria del Giglio landing stage on the left, the **Palazzo Pisani-Gritti ㉑** belonged to Doge Andrea Gritti in the 16th century. The palace became a hotel between the wars and has a roll-call of illustrious visitors. Soon after the Gritti is the tiny **Ca' Contarini-Fasan ㉒**, known as the House of Desdemona.

Grand finale

Standing guard near the canal entrance is the **Santa Maria della Salute ㉓** (see page 58), Longhena's Baroque masterpiece with a huge, exuberant façade and massive dome.

Just past it, on the tip of the promontory, the figure of Fortuna on a golden globe adorns the top of the **Punta della Dogana ㉔** (Campo San Samuele, tel: 041-523 1680; for tickets tel: +39 0445 230 313 from abroad; www.palazzograssi.it; Wed–Mon 10am–7pm), the former customs house, currently home to François Pinault's fabulous 2,500-strong contemporary art collection. Redesigned by Tadao Ando, the ravishing gallery (housed in the Palazzo Grassi) has helped turn this stretch of Dorsoduro into the so-called 'art mile', running down to the Guggenheim.

Stay on the boat until the landing stage at **San Zaccaria ㉕** to enjoy the stunning view of the San Marco waterfront, as well as the island of San Giorgio, before disembarking.

Food and Drink

❶ IL MURO

San Polo 222, Campo Bella Vienna (labelled Campo Battisti on maps); tel: 041-241 2339; www.murovinoecucina.it; daily; €

Il Muro makes a friendly stop for sparkling wine, cocktails and *cicchetti*, or for a full meal, with outdoor tables by the Rialto.

❷ NARANZARIA

San Polo 130, Erberia; tel: 041-724 1035; www.naranzaria.it; Tue–Sun; €€

This contemporary *osteria-enoteca* with Grand Canal views occupies a former citrus fruit warehouse. Expect fresh seafood, fusion dishes and sushi.

❸ AL BANCOGIRO

San Polo 122, Erberia/Campo San Giacometto; tel: 041-523 2061; www.osteriabancogiro.it; Tue–Sun; €€

This wine bar and new-wave *bacaro* stands on the site of the city's earliest bank. Offers *cicchetti* and a creative menu.

View of the Grand Canal and La Salute from the Ponte dell'Accademia

THE ACCADEMIA

This treasury of Venetian art ranges from Renaissance masterpieces and Byzantine panels to ceremonial paintings, but it is as memorable for its snapshots of everyday life as for its sumptuous showpieces. Ideally combine a gallery visit with a walk around Dorsoduro (route 7).

TIME: 2–3 hours
START/END: Entrance to the Accademia
POINTS TO NOTE: The paintings are dependent on natural light, so choose a bright morning and arrive early. Otherwise, aim for late afternoon to avoid crowds or reserve tickets at www.gallerie accademia.org. At time of writing the gallery's information sheets were in Italian, so you may want to hire an audio guide (€5). New refurbished gallery spaces, where paintings from the 17th- to the 20th century will be displayed, are currently on view Thur–Sun 10am–5pm, along with Palladio's Great Couryard.

The collection of the **Gallerie dell'Accademia** (Galleries of the Accademia, Campo della Carità; www.gallerieacca demia.org; Mon 8.15am–2pm, Tue–Sun 8.15am–7.15pm; charge) is housed in Santa Maria della Carità, a complex of church, convent, cloisters and charitable confraternity. The church was deconsecrated in Napoleonic times and became a repository of work created during the Venetian Republic.

It is the world's finest collection of Venetian paintings, notable for vibrant colour, luminosity and a supreme decorative sense. It spans five centuries and includes work by Mantegna, Bellini, Giorgione, Carpaccio, Titian, Tintoretto, Veronese and Tiepolo.

The art is loosely arranged in chronological order, from the 14th to 18th centuries though Rooms 20–23 with early Renaissance masterpieces are out of sequence. The gallery is undergoing a major restructure and expansion, so paintings are being shuffled around, and some rooms (eg XII–XVI) are completely closed off. The whole of the first floor (14th–16th centuries) is also due to be refurbished.

BYZANTINE STYLE

Room I shows the influence of the Byzantine on the early Venetian painters. The main exponent in Venice was Paolo Veneziano, whose *Coronation of the Virgin*, the polyptych facing you as you

The Accademia also hosts temporary exhibitions

enter Room I. Further down on the left, Michele Giambono's *Coronation of the Virgin*, with detailed rendering of figures, is a fine example of the International Gothic style.

VENETIAN RENAISSANCE

Rooms II–IV are dominated by Giovanni Bellini, his school and the early Venetian Renaissance. Renaissance painting came late to Venice, chiefly introduced by Andrea Mantegna (Bellini's brother-in-law).

Bellini family

Giovanni Bellini ('Giambellino') is considered the founder of the Venetian school. He broke away from the traditional polyptych and brought the Virgin and saints together in a single natural composition called the *Sacra Conversazione* (Sacred Conversation). His *Madonna Enthroned with Saints* in Room II heavily influenced Carpaccio's *Presentation of Jesus in the Temple* and Marco Basaiti's *Agony in the Garden*, both hanging in the same room.

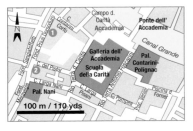

'Giambellino' was the greatest of the Venetian Madonna painters. Along with his father, Gentile, and brother, Jacopo, he commanded a large workshop that churned out these devotional paintings. His *Madonna and Child with St Catherine and St Mary Magdalene* in Room IV demonstrates his masterly balance of grace, realism and harmony.

Room V should also display masterpieces by Giovanni Bellini, including the sublime Madonna and Child with John the Baptist and a Saint, demonstrating the artist's ability to bring together figures and landscape in perfect harmony. Bellini's paintings are not all idealised Madonnas. In his poignant Pietà, the suffering Virgin cradles her son, her careworn face a testament to the painter's expressive powers.

Titian, Veronese and Tintoretto

Rooms VI–VIII pave the way for the High Renaissance works of art, introducing Titian, Tintoretto and Veronese. Titian (c.1487–1576) dominated Venetian painting throughout his long life. Brilliant use of colour and lyrical composition are the hallmarks of his genius. His *St John the Baptist* in Room VIII is boldly presented as a muscular athlete in a theatrical pose.

Typical of the first half of the 16th century are the richly coloured, exuberant paintings such as the *Sacra Conversazione* by Palma Il Vecchio, also in **Room VIII**. On an entirely different note is the melancholic yet penetrating *Por-*

trait of a Young Man by Lorenzo Lotto in the adjoining room. Acute observation of personality is a notable feature of Venetian Renaissance portraiture.

Take the steps up to **Room X** for the masterpieces of the High Renaissance. Paolo Caliari (1528–88), better known as Veronese, as he was from Verona, painted with verve and realism. Covering one entire wall is his grandiose *Feast in the House of Levi*. It depicted *The Last Supper* but its hedonistic content (including dogs, drunkards and dwarfs) brought Veronese before the Inquisition. Rather than eliminate the offending details, however, the painter merely changed the title of the work.

Tintoretto (1518–94) was born in Venice and never moved from her shores. Most of his work remains in the city. A man of fervent faith, he brought a kind of frenetic Mannerism to the Renaissance. His reputation was made with the striking *St Mark Rescuing the Slave*. Inspired use of shadow, foreshortening, depth and movement are typified in the dramatic *Stealing of the Body of St Mark* and *St Mark Saving a Saracen from Shipwreck*.

In the same room, Titian's dark and poignant *Pietà*, bathed in mystic light, was the artist's last gasp, painted when he was over 90 years old, possibly for his own tomb in the Frari. Veronese's *Marriage of St Catherine* and *Madonna Enthroned with Saints* are radiant, richly coloured works demonstrating his use of dazzling hues.

Tiepolo

Room XI features further works by Tintoretto and introduces Tiepolo with fresco lunettes on the upper levels. At the far end of the room you can't miss his *Discovery of the True Cross*, showing his mastery of illusionistic perspective. Rooms XII–XIX are undergoing restoration, and most the works previously displayed here will be hung in the new galleries.

Canaletto

Venice was beloved by Grand Tourists, notably the English, French and Germans, who became collectors of Venetian keepsakes, of which the most prized were paintings. Canaletto was the most popular export, thanks to his English patron, Josef Smith. Only three of his paintings remain in Venice. His *Perspective*, the only Canaletto in the Accademia, is a good example of his precisely drawn, perspectively accurate scenes.

CEREMONIAL ART

The Republic set great store by the State painter, with artists of the calibre of Bellini, Titian and Tintoretto expected to capture Venetian glory with vibrant depictions of ceremonial events, such as the receiving of prelates, ambassadors and dignitaries. Rooms XX and XXI take you back in time, featuring two great cycles of paintings from the late 15th and early 16th centuries *The Stories of the True Cross* (Room XX), eight large canvasses by five leading 'ceremonial artists', pro-

Detail of Veronese's Feast in the House of Levi (1573)

vide a fascinating glimpse of the life, customs and appearance of Venice at the time. Worth singling out are Gentile Bellini's *Corpus Domini Procession*, showing Piazza San Marco and (opposite) *The Curing of a Man Possessed by Demons* by Carpaccio, showing the old wooden Rialto Bridge, which collapsed in 1524.

Room XXI is devoted to Carpaccio's intimate yet wonderfully graphic *Scenes from the Life of St Ursula*, using settings and costumes of 15th-century Venice. The cycle depicts the tragic life of this Breton heroine; her acceptance of the hand of the British prince, Hereus, on condition he converts to Christianity, their subsequent pilgrimage to Rome and her eventual martyrdom.

CONVENT CHAPEL

Room XXIII is the original chapel, now finely restored as a gallery. It now showcases some of the great highlights of the Accademia (moved from Rooms IV and V). Giorgione's *Tempest* was a high point of the Venetian Renaissance. Little is known about the artist, who died of the plague in his early 30s, but he is ranked as one of the founders of modern painting. He trained under Bellini and was an innovator in that he achieved his effect through the use of colour and light as opposed to line and drawing. *The Tempest* is one of his few certain attributions, but the subject still remains a mystery. Beside it, *The Old Woman*, by the same artist, is a striking piece of early realism. Another Renaissance masterpiece that has been moved here is Bellini's *Madonna of the Little Trees* (formerly in Room V).

The **Sala Grande (XXIV)**, the restored last room, is a work of art in itself. Also known as the Sala dell'Albergo, the former confraternity hall has a coffered ceiling and a triptych by Antonio Vivarini and Giovanni d'Alemagna, which charts the transition from International Gothic to Renaissance. Titian's *Presentation of the Virgin*, on the entrance wall of the gallery, makes a fitting finale.

Once you've had your fill of art, satisfy your hunger at **Taverna San Trovaso**, see ❶ or try tasty *chichetti* and wines at Lo Squero, see ❷.

Food and Drink

❶ RISTORANTE SAN TROVASO

Dorsoduro 967, Fondamenta Priuli; tel: 041-520 3703; Fri–Wed noon-3.30pm and 7–9.45pm; €€

This traditional Dorsoduro eatery draws many regulars for straightforward, affordable trattoria fare.

❷ AL SQUERO

Dorsoduro 943-944; Fondamenta Meraveglie; tel: 335 600 7513; www.osteria lsquero.it; Tue–Sun 9am–9.30pm; €

This little osteria overlooking Squero San Trovaso boatyard serves a first-class spritz, delicious *cicchetti* and a selection of *prosciutto crudo* and cheese.

Opulent La Fenice

THE SESTIERE OF SAN MARCO

There's more to the sestiere of San Marco than its showpiece Piazza. The district is home to imposing churches, the Fenice theatre and the parade of palazzi that flank the southern curve of the Grand Canal.

DISTANCE: 3km (2 miles)
TIME: 2–3 hours
START/END: Piazza San Marco
POINTS TO NOTE: This route makes a great add-on to Piazza San Marco (see page 28).

Leave **Piazza San Marco** ❶ (see page 28) at the western end, under the arch all the way to the left. Salizzada San Moisè leads to the church of San Moisè. Cross the bridge to the Calle Larga XXII Marzo, a broad upmarket shopping street, whose name refers to the day (22 March) when patriots reclaimed the Republic from the Austrians during the 1848 uprising.

AROUND LA FENICE

Campo San Fantin
Divert right along Calle della Veste (marked Calle del Sartor da Veste), over the bridge and into Campo San Fantin. If you're ready for a Venetian lunch on the run, consider stopping in **Vino Vino**, see ❶, right before you enter the Campo. To

your right is the late Renaissance church of San Fantin, to the left the rebuilt **Teatro La Fenice** ❷ (Campo San Fantin; reserve guided tours daily from 9.30am–6pm at the ticket office or tel: 041-2424; charge), whose neoclassical facade hides one of the world's loveliest opera auditoria. In 1938 it was almost completely destroyed by fire, but rose again 'like a phoenix' *(fenice)*, rebuilt almost exactly as before. Fire struck again in 1996. This time restorers were running up large debts for failing to complete the work on time, and two electricians were sentenced for arson, even if conspiracy theorists are unconvinced. After eight years of rebuilding, the theatre was faithfully restored to its former glory. The reopening in 2004 was celebrated with a gala performance of Verdi's *La Traviata*.

Campo Santa Maria del Giglio
Take Calle de la Fenice on the right side of the theatre, go left under the colonnade and cross the bridge. Turn left into little Campiello dei Calegheri, over the bridge and along the Fondamenta della Fenice, where you can see the water entrance

Baroque San Moisè   *Santa Maria del Giglio statue*

to the opera house. The first right turning leads you into **Campo Santa Maria del Giglio ❸**, whose church of the same name (Mon–Sat 10am–5pm; Chorus Church, see page 125; charge or book a Chorus pass on www.chorusvenezia.org), with its profusion of Baroque ornamentation and secular statuary, appalled the art historian John Ruskin. Also here is Rubens' *Madonna with Child and St John* (in the chapel on the right).

CAMPO SAN MAURIZIO

Turn right out of the square, cross over two bridges to **Campo San Maurizio**, following the yellow sign for the Accademia. The former Church of San Maurizio is home to the Museo della Musica (Music Museum; daily 10am–7pm), with a collection of rare musical instruments and an exhibition on Vivaldi.

CAMPO SANTO STEFANO

The narrow Calle Spezier brings you to the large Campo Santo Stefano. Enjoy the bustle from one of the open-air cafés, such as **Le Café**, see **❷**. Bull-baiting took place in the square until 1802, when several spectators were killed by a falling stand.

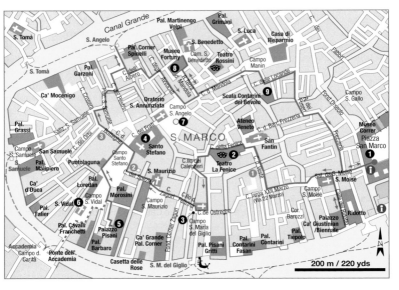

Busy Campo Santo Stefano

The fine Gothic church, **Santo Stefano** ❹ (Mon–Sat 10am–5pm, Sun 1–5pm; charge for sacristy), has a splendid ship's-keel roof and an inconspicuous sacristy packed with dark paintings by Tintoretto and other Venetian masters.

Off the southern end of the Campo, the massive **Palazzo Pisani** ❺ houses the Conservatory of Music, where melodious strains often waft from open windows. The deconsecrated church of **San Vidal** ❻ on the eponymous square is the setting of regular Vivaldi concerts by the highly rated Interpreti Veneziani (www.interpretiveneziani.com). Just beyond the square make a brief detour to the **Accademia Bridge** for great views of the Grand Canal and church of La Salute church.

Return to Campo Santo Stefano and take the slim Calle delle Botteghe opposite the church, past shops, galleries and authentic inns such as **Fiore**, see ❸.

CAMPO SANT'ANGELO

Turn right down the Ramo di Piscina for the Piscina San Samuele. Take the steps up and cross two bridges for the Corte de l'Albero and access to the Grand Canal. The quayside here by the Sant' Angelo landing stage affords fine views of the palazzi opposite.

Back at Corte del' Albero, take the narrow street on the far side of the square and turn right down Calle degli Avvocati for **Campo Sant'Angelo** ❼, a noble quarter lined with palaces, where Casanova (see box) played his practical jokes. From here you can't fail to notice the alarming tilt of Santo Stefano's campanile.

MUSEO FORTUNY

Turn left into Calle Spezier (marked Rialto). A diversion marked to the left leads to the late-Gothic Palazzo Fortuny, former home of Mariano Fortuny. The Catalan artist, sculptor and set designer spent much of his life in this

---

Casanova's Venice

Not merely an arch seducer, Casanova (1725–98) was also an adventurer, gambler, soldier, spy, musician and man of letters. In 1755, he was arrested on charges of freemasonry and licentiousness, but daringly escaped from prison. He led a clandestine existence until returning to Venice in 1774, acting as a spy for the Venetian Inquisition. His Venice is still largely intact: you can see his birthplace in the romantic San Samuele quarter, or visit Campo Sant'Angelo, where he indulged in childish pranks, untying moored gondolas or summoning sleeping midwives and priests to imaginary emergencies. From his home, the city's finest clubs and salons were within easy walking distance, including gambling dens in the Frezzeria such as the Ridotto, the casino where Casanova learnt his trade.

The exquisite Scala Contarini del Bovolo

palace. The pleated Fortuny silk dresses for which he is famed became the rage in the early 20th century. The renovated palace houses the **Museo Fortuny** ❽ (Campo San Bento 3958; www.fortuny. visitmuve.it; Wed–Mon 10am–6pm; charge), which displays Fortuny's atelier and fabrics, as well as changing displays devoted to design, costumes or contemporary art.

CAMPO MANIN

Returning to the main Rialto route, you come to **Campo Manin**. A statue of Daniele Manin, who led the Venetian uprising against the Austrians in 1848, stands with his back to the Cassa di Risparmio bank, looking towards the house he lived in when the rebellion was plotted.

Scala Contarini
Take the tiny street right off the Campo, signposted to the **Scala Contarini del Bovolo** ❾ (Calle delle Locande 4299; closed for restoration, www.scalabovolo. org), a jewel of a stairway that spirals up the Palazzo Contarini del Bovolo. (*Bovolo* in Venetian dialect means snail shell.) It's worth a detour, even during restoration, since the best bit is the exterior.

BACK TO SAN MARCO

Turn right along Calle delle Locande and right again into Calle dei Fuseri to the **Frezzeria**, the busiest shopping street

in Venice. Named after the arrow makers who had workshops here, it was notorious for prostitutes, but is now home to an array of superior crafts and tourist tat. A left turn takes you back via the Salizzada San Moisè to Calle del Ridotto, and a Prosecco at the Ombra del Leone (see page 35).

Food and Drink

❶ VINO VINO
San Marco 2007/A, Ponte delle Veste; tel: 041-241 7688; www.vinovinowinebar.com; daily 11.30am–11.30pm; cash only; €€
Charming annexe to the Antico Martini restaurant, this cosy inn serves fine wines by the glass, and hearty *cicchetti*. Brusque service is the only downside.

❷ LE CAFÉ
San Marco 2797, Campo Santo Stefano; tel: 041-523 7201; daily; €–€€
This café serves delicious cakes and sandwiches and is a good spot for sipping an alfresco spritz before dinner.

❸ FIORE
San Marco 3461, Calle delle Botteghe; tel: 041-523 5310; www.dafiore.it; Wed–Mon; €€
This cosy *trattoria* is good value considering its chic setting. It is divided into a *bacaro* with a wide array of *cicchetti* and a small restaurant that specialises in seasonal Venetian cuisine.

Gondolas moored along the Riva degli Schiavoni

WESTERN CASTELLO

Lying to the north and east of San Marco, Castello – the largest sestiere in Venice – offers a mix of sophistication and sleepy charm. Beyond the bustle of Riva degli Schiavoni, the western side offers a slice of everyday Venetian life and some of the city's finest art and architectural treasures.

DISTANCE: 1.5km (1 mile)
TIME: 2–3 hours
START: Molo
END: Santi Giovanni e Paolo
POINTS TO NOTE: This route can be combined with no. 11 (in reverse) via a short walk to Santa Maria dei Miracoli.

THE MOLO

Start at the **Molo ❶**, the waterfront to the south of the Doge's Palace, where gondolas sway by the quayside and crowds admire the views across the water to the island of San Giorgio Maggiore. Head through stalls of souvenirs and cross the Ponte della Paglia. Look left for the **Ponte dei Sospiri** (Bridge of Sighs; see page 33).

Riva degli Schiavoni

Now cross a bridge to the mercantile **Riva degli Schiavoni**, a long, curving promenade skirting the *sestiere* of Castello, and named after the Dalmatian sailors who used to moor their boats

and barges along the waterfront. It is still a scene of intense activity, as vaporetti, *motoscafi*, barges, tugs and cruisers moor at the landing stages, and ferries chug across to the islands. The Riva is lined with distinguished hotels, the most historic of which is the **Hotel Danieli** (see page 99).

SAN ZACCARIA

Cross the colonnaded Ponte del Vin and take the second turning to the left, under the *sottoportego* (covered passageway) signposted to San Zaccaria. This brings you to a quiet campo, flanked on one side by the part-Gothic and part-Renaissance facade of the church of **San Zaccaria ❷** (Mon–Sat 10am–noon, 4–6pm, Sun 4–6pm). The upper section, by leading Renaissance architect Mauro Coducci, has been well restored. In the 16th century the adjoining convent – not unlike other convents in the city – was notorious for its riotous, amoral nuns.

Inside the church, start with the chapels and (often flooded) crypt, reached by an entrance on the right-hand side. The

Canal near San Lorenzo

San Giorgio dei Greci

Chapel of St Athanasius (charge), with paintings by Palma Vecchio, Titian and Tintoretto, leads to the Capella di San Tarasio, the former chancel. The Vivarini family executed the glorious altarpieces, with their ornate gilded frames, which are a fine example of the Gothic painting style that was in fashion before the Renaissance took hold in Venice.

The greatest work of art – Giovanni Bellini's glorious Madonna and Child with Saints (1505) is in the main church, above the second altarpiece on the left. Here, Bellini created a new type of religious painting, not based on a story from the Bible, but rather a scene in which serene, meditative figures gather for a 'Sacra Conversazione' (Holy Conversation), embraced by soft shadow and rich, mellow hues.

It is hard to associate the peaceful Campo San Zaccaria with its reputation for skulduggery and licence. Three doges were assassinated in the vicinity, while the adjoining Benedictine convent was a byword for lascivious living. Noblewomen were often despatched to nunneries to save money on dowries, so tales of libertine nuns were rife.

SCUOLA DI SAN GIORGIO DEGLI SCHIAVONI

Leave the square via the archway. Turn right into Campo San Provolo, go under the *sottoportego* and you will come into the charming quayside of **Fondamenta dell'Osmarin**. On a corner on the far side of the canal is the red-brick Palazzo Priuli, a fine Venetian Gothic palace. At the end of the canal cross the two bridges and look right to the Greek Orthodox church of **San Giorgio dei Greci** distinguished by its dome and tall, tilting bell tower. Take the narrow alley straight ahead, pass Campiello della Fraterna on the left, and join Salizzada dei Greci. The **Trattoria da Remigio**, see ➊, is a good option for an authentic lunch.

At the far end of the street cross over the bridge and turn left. Follow the canal along the Fondamenta dei Furlani for the **Scuola di San Giorgio degli Schiavoni** ➌ (Calle dei Furiani 3259A; Mon 2.45–6pm, Tue–Sat 9.15am–1pm, 2.30–6pm, Sun 9.15am–1pm; variable slightly reduced hours in low season; charge), founded by the Slavs from Dalmatia to protect their community in Venice. This was one of the city's several *scuole*, charitable lay associations that looked after members' spiritual, moral and material welfare. Serving the citizen class from lawyers and merchants to skilled artisans, the *scuole* were expected to support the State and contribute to good causes.

The tiny Scuola is decorated with an exquisite frieze of paintings by Carpaccio, illustrating the lives of the Dalmatian patron saints, St George, St Tryphon and St Jerome. The scenes are rich in colour, remarkably vivid and detailed, giving a good idea of life in Venice in the early 16th century.

Stained glass in San Zanipolo

SANTA MARIA FORMOSA

Coming out of the Scuola, cross the bridge and turn right, following the canal northwards. Shortly before a portico, take a left turn down the Calle San Lorenzo for the church of San Lorenzo, now a hospice. Marco Polo is said to have been buried here, but his tomb was lost when the church was rebuilt in 1592.

Cross the bridge at the other side of the square, turn immediately right, then first left down the Borgoloco San Lorenzo. Cross the canal of San Severo, pausing on the bridge to see some fine *palazzi*, pass under the dark and narrow *sottoportego*, carry straight on, then take a right turn for the lovely **Campo Santa Maria Formosa**.

This charming, rambling square, once the site of bullfights and masked balls, is full of Venetian life, with market stalls and open-air cafés. It is flanked by *palazzi* and dominated by the swelling apses of Coducci's church of **Santa Maria Formosa** ❹ (Mon–Sat 10am–5pm, Sun 1–5pm; charge). Don't miss Palma il Vecchio's polyptych of *St Barbara and Saints*, adorning the chapel of the Scuola dei Bombardieri. The same artist painted portraits of Francesco and Paolo Querini, who

St Barbara and Saints, Santa Formosa

built the 16th-century Querini-Stampalia palace south of the square. Today the building houses the **Fondazione Querini-Stampalia** ❺ (Tue–Sun 10am–6pm,; www.quirinistampalia.it; charge), comprising a gallery of Venetian paintings, a library, garden, café, and a splendid room where concerts of Baroque music are staged.

If you didn't stop for lunch earlier, the convivial **Al Mascaròn** (see page 109), is tucked away in Calle Lunga Santa Maria Formosa, the narrow street just east of the square.

Take the tiny street almost opposite Al Mascaròn, cross the quiet canal and go straight on for Campo Santi Giovanni e Paolo.

CAMPO SAN ZANIPOLO

The church of **Santi Giovanni e Paolo** ❻ (Mon–Sat 9am–6pm, Sun noon–6pm; charge) is better known as San Zanipolo. This huge brick edifice vies with the Frari as the city's greatest Gothic church. Known as the Pantheon of Venice, it contains the tombs of 25 doges. Artistic highlights include Giovanni Bellini's *St Vincent Ferrer polyptych*, over the second altar on the right, and the Veronese ceiling paintings in the Rosary Chapel.

Scuola Grande di San Marco

The unadorned facade of Zanipolo is flanked by the ornate **Scuola Grande di San Marco** ❼, once the meeting house of silk-dealers and goldsmiths, now the civic hospital (ambulances are usually moored in the adjoining canal). Either side of the entrance, the *trompe l'oeil* arches frame lions that appear to be looking from the far end of deep Renaissance porticos – in fact they are barely 15cm (6in) deep. At the end of the route, relax in the **Antico Caffè Rosa Salva**, see ❷.

The great Renaissance gateway

EASTERN CASTELLO

This leisurely stroll takes you through eastern Castello, a workaday quarter far removed from the madding crowds of San Marco, taking in a variety of lesser-known sights. As this area is rarely crowded, except during the Biennale, this route is ideal for those looking to escape the masses.

DISTANCE: 2.5km (1.5 miles)
TIME: 2 hours
START: Arsenale landing stage
END: Giardini landing stage
POINTS TO NOTE: Between the Arsenale, Museo Storico Navale and Giardini Pubblici, this route is great for families. You can arrive at the Arsenale landing via vapore 1, 4.1, 4.2 and 2.

THE ARSENALE

From the **Arsenale landing stage ❶**, east of San Marco, turn right (as you face inland), cross the bridge and turn immediately left. Stop on the wooden bridge over the Rio dell'Arsenale for the best views of the entrance to the **Arsenale ❷**, the old Venetian shipyard that became the symbol of Venetian maritime might. Heralding the shipyard is the great Renaissance gateway, guarded by stone lions plundered from Piraeus, the great shipyard in Athens, Greece. Beside the triumphal arch is a relief of Dante and a plaque record-

ing his reference to the Arsenale in *The Divine Comedy*. The writer came here in 1306 and 1321, and the scene of frenzied activity left a lasting impression.

Naval History Museum

Back on the main waterfront stands the dignified **Museo Storico Navale ❸** (Campo San Biagio; Mon–Fri 8.45am–1.30pm, Sat 8.45am–1pm; charge). Given the tantalising elusiveness of the Arsenale, the Naval History Museum is the only place where you can fully appreciate the greatness of maritime Venice. Before its present incarnation, the 16th-century building was used as a naval granary and biscuit warehouse. Models of Venetian craft include the original gondolas, complete with *felze* or cabin (the 'shelter of sweet sins'), and a replica of the lavish *Bucintoro*, the doge's state barge.

AROUND VIA GARIBALDI

Beyond the next bridge turn inland for the **Via Garibaldi ❹**. The widest street in Venice, it was created by Napoleon

Rio di Sant'Anna   *Arsenale shipyard*

in 1808 by filling in the canal here. The first house on the right, marked with a plaque, was home to the Italian explorers and navigators John Cabot and his son Sebastian, who discovered the Labrador coast of Newfoundland (mistaken at the time as the coast of China) for the English crown. The street is lined with basic grocery shops, food stalls and friendly bars and restaurants. If you're looking to grab a glass of wine, try the small **El Refolo**, see ❶, where clients spill out onto the street.

On the right you soon come to the **Giardini Pubblici** (Public Gardens) fronted by a bronze monument to the revolutionary leader Garibaldi. Keep straight ahead for the Rio di Sant'Anna, where you will find one of the last surviving floating vegetable markets in the city. Take the first turning on the left (marked Calle San Gioachino). A little bridge crosses a canal festooned with laundry and flanked by brightly coloured boats. Cross a bridge into Calle Riello and then turn left for Campo di Ruga, and beyond the square on Salizada Stretta take the second turning on the right and cross the bridge for the island of San Pietro.

THE ISLAND OF SAN PIETRO

The beautiful but seriously listing campanile in front of you was the work of Mauro

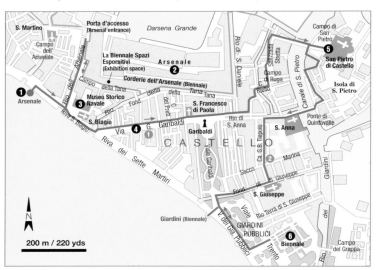

The Canale di San Pietro

Coducci in 1482–8. This is the bell tower for **San Pietro di Castello** ❺ (Mon–Sat 10am–5pm; Chorus Church, see page 125; charge, www.chorusvenezia.org). It seems remarkable that this remote church, set on a grassy square, was the Venetian seat of religious power. It was built to a Palladian design in 1557 on the site of a former castle (hence 'Castello'). Until 1807, when the bishop (later patriarch) was transferred to the Basilica of San Marco, this was Venice's cathedral.

Food and Drink

❶ EL REFOLO

Castello 1580, Via Garibaldi; tel: 346 5235 837; Tue–Sun 10.30am–12.30am or later; €

This *enoteca* is tiny, but what it lacks in space, it makes up for in warmth. Expect unusual wines and imaginative sandwiches made with wild boar mortadella or Alpine cheeses, as well as *bigoli in salsa* (buckwheat pasta in an anchovy and onion sauce). No reservations or credit cards.

❷ DAI TOSI

Castello 738, Secco Marina; tel: 041-523 7102; Thur–Tue; €

This simple *trattoria* and pizzeria comes into its own during the Biennale, as the exhibition is staged in the nearby Giardini. Outside the Biennale, Dai Tosi attracts a younger crowd, drawn to the pizzas and keen to dine in the garden in summer.

Take the path behind the Campanile and recross the Canale di San Pietro over the Ponte di Quintavalle bridge. From here you can see boatyards and fishing smacks. Pass the monastery of **Sant'Anna**, on your left, then take the first left. Carry straight on and then turn left onto Secco Marina, where you will find the favourite local eatery, **Dai Tosi**, see ❷, a good place to stop for a spot of lunch. This is a working-class neighbourhood, and you are likely to be eating with more local people than tourists.

From the Fondamenta San Giuseppe, turn right, heading south to the main waterfront and Giardini Pubblici. Boat enthusiasts will enjoy the waterfront here, as gondolas, tugs, yachts and Lido ferries ply the waters of the inner lagoon.

LA BIENNALE

If you are here in an odd-numbered year between June and November, join the art crowd at the **Biennale** ❻. Around 30 permanent and another 60 temporary pavilions in the gardens display contemporary art from different nations. Although for much of the rest of the time the pavilions remain empty, they are now used for other events such as the Biennale dell'Architettura, which is held in the intervening years between September and November.

From the Giardini landing stage, jump onto a No. 4.2 or a No 1 vaporetto going westwards and enjoy the views as you head back to San Marco.

Church of the Gesuati

DORSODURO

Dorsoduro means 'hard back', so called because the district occupies the largest area of firm land in Venice. Stroll along its Zattere quayside, visit galleries in the area's chic eastern quarter, then retreat to one of Venice's liveliest squares. End by going off the beaten track to visit two of the city's loveliest churches.

DISTANCE: 3.5km (2.25 miles)
TIME: 4–5 hours
START: Zattere landing stage
END: San Basilio landing stage
POINTS TO NOTE: This route can be combined with San Giorgio and the Giudecca (route 8) by taking the No. 2 vaporetto from the Giudecca Palanca stop to the Zattere.

Apart from the Accademia and La Salute basilica, Dorsoduro is surprisingly quiet, even if the creation of new art galleries along the Zattere has confirmed the area as a hub for contemporary art.

THE ZATTERE

Start at the **Zattere landing stage ❶**, serviced by waterbus No. 2, 5.1 and 5.2. The Zattere, which means floating rafts, from the days when cargo was off-loaded here, is a quayside awash with art galleries and open-air cafés such as **Nico**, see ❶. From here, turn right onto the Fondamenta Nani, which offers fine views, across the canal, of the **Squero di San Trovaso ❷**, one of the last surviving gondola yards.

The next stop on the Zattere is the **Gesuati ❸** (Mon–Sat 10am–5pm; Chorus Church, see page 125; charge), just east of the landing stage. The church is a supreme example of 18th-century Venetian architecture, and holds Tiepolo masterpieces in their original setting (1739).

Further along the Zattere is Pensione **La Calcina**, otherwise known as Ruskin's House. The art historian stayed here when it was a simple inn, frequented by artists.

Follow the quayside, past the Casa degli Incurabili, a former hospice, to the **Magazzini del Sale ❹**, the Salt Warehouses that helped found 15th-century Venetian fortunes. These are now used for art exhibitions and events, as is the sister space, revamped by Renzo Piano, the **Fondazione Vedova** (www.fondazionevedova.org for both venues; Wed–Mon 10.30am–6pm during exhibitions; charge). Stop for refreshment at the adjacent **Linea d'Ombra** (see page 111).

Santa Maria della Salute

Punta della Dogana

Commanding the point is the **Punta della Dogana ❺** (Wed–Mon 10am–7pm; charge), a cutting-edge showcase for contemporary art, belonging to French businessman and art collector François Pinault and restored by Japanese architect Tadao Ando.

Designed like a ship's prow, this 17th-century Customs House is crowned by two bronze Atlases bearing a golden globe, with the weathervane figure of Fortuna on top. Striking contemporary sculptures also adorn the quaysides. The Punta della Dogana forms an integral whole with the Palazzo Grassi, further down the Grand Canal (see page 40), and, for conservative Venice, is a bold new step.

SANTA MARIA DELLA SALUTE

Rounding the peninsula, you come to Longhena's monumental church of **Santa Maria della Salute ❻** (Campo della Salute; 9am–noon, 3–6.30pm, until 5.30pm in winter; church free, charge for sacristy), erected to commemorate the deliverance of Venice from the plague of 1630. On 21 November the event is celebrated at the Feast of the Salute when a pontoon bridge is laid down over the

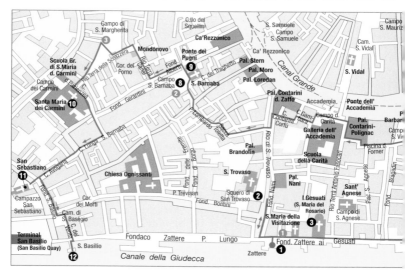

The Guggenheim Collection   *Campo San Vio*

Grand Canal, linking La Salute with San Marco, and Venetians traditionally cross the bridge to light candles and give thanks for good health. A Baroque church of massive proportions, it took over half a century to build and is supported by over a million timber piles. After the exuberance of the facade, the grey-and-white interior is surprisingly severe. The highlights are the works by Titian in the sacristy.

THE GUGGENHEIM

Back in Campo della Salute, cross the tiny bridge to the Campo San Gregorio, where the deconsecrated Gothic brick church of **San Gregorio** is now used as a workshop for restoring paintings. Continue to the little Campiello Barbaro, overlooked by the ill-fated Palazzo Ca' Dario (see page 40) and on over a bridge to the Palazzo Venier dei Leoni, housing the **Peggy Guggenheim Collection** ❼ (www.guggenheim-venice.it; Wed–Mon 10am–6pm; charge). Peggy Guggenheim (1898–1979), the eccentric American heiress, bought the palace in 1949 and lived here until her death.

The city's most-visited gallery after the Accademia, it has a collection featuring works from almost every modern art movement of the 20th century, plus a sculpture garden and good café. The majority of the works came directly from the artists, many of whom she patronised, befriended, entertained and – in the case of Max Ernst – married. Picasso, Pollock, Magritte, Mondrian, Brancusi and Giacometti are just a few of the big names.

CAMPO SAN VIO

Following the route eastwards along the Fondamenta Venier dei Leoni you come to a bridge and the long-established restaurant, **Ai Gondolieri** (see page 110). Campo San Vio beyond is one of those rare Venetian squares where you can sit on a bench and lap up the bustle of the Grand Canal. From here it's an easy stroll to Campo della Carità and the **Accademia** (see page 42).

200 m / 220 yds

Student-haunt Campo San Barnaba

WESTERN DORSODURO

From Campo della Carità, zigzag along the streets beyond the Accademia, and cross the Rio di San Trovaso at the first bridge. Follow the flow to **Campo San Barnaba** ⑧, passing artisans' studios. Once home to the impoverished nobility, today the district is dominated by students; join them by stopping for an ice cream at **Grom**, see ②.

Exit from the north end of the square, turning left onto Fondamenta Gerardini and crossing the **Ponte dei Pugni** ⑨ (Bridge of Fists). At the foot of the bridge you'll see a colourful barge crammed with fresh fruit and vegetables – one of the last of Venice's floating markets.

The Carmini and San Sebastiano

Carry on down Rio Terrà Canal and bear left for Campo di Santa Margherita. The square bustles with life and is normally full of students from the nearby Ca' Foscari University. **Bar Margaret Duchamp**, see ③, is especially good for people-watching.

At the far end of the square is the church and *Scuola* Grande of the **Carmini** ⑩ (Campo Carmini; church: Mon–Sat 2.30–5.30pm; free; *Scuola*: daily 11am–4pm; charge). The *scuola* houses Tiepolo's ceiling painting of *St Simon Stock Receiving the Scapula of the Carmelite Order from the Virgin*.

From here, go right down Calle della Pazienza, cross the first bridge, then turn right onto Calle Lunga San Barnaba, leading to the church of **San Sebastiano** ⑪ (Mon–Sat 10am–5pm; charge), reached across a tiny bridge. The church is a virtual museum of Paolo Veronese, its ceilings, frieze, choir, altar, organ doors and sacristy decorated with the artist's glowing and joyous works of art. This was Veronese's parish church, and, fittingly, he is buried here.

Cross the bridge out of the square and follow Fondamenta San Basilio south to the Zattere. A No. 2 vaporetto from **San Basilio** ⑫ will take you back to San Marco or via the Stazione Marittima towards the north of the city.

Food and Drink

① NICO

Dorsoduro 922, Zattere; tel: 041-522 5293; Fri–Wed; €
Nico is the best place to buy a *gelato* to eat while strolling along the waterfront.

② GROM

Dorsoduro 2461, Campo San Barnaba; tel: 041-241 3531; daily; €
This purist Piedmontese ice-cream chain only uses the freshest ingredients, from Piedmontese hazelnuts to Amalfi lemons.

③ MARGARET DUCHAMP

Dorsoduro 3019, Campo di Santa Margherita; tel: 041-528 6255; daily; €
One of the best-known bars on the square, perfect for a coffee or spritz in the sun.

Majestic San Giorgio Maggiore

SAN GIORGIO MAGGIORE AND THE GIUDECCA

Enjoy vistas of Venetian landmarks, as the vaporetto chugs across the Canal of San Marco to the island of San Giorgio Maggiore. Then head towards the Giudecca, taking in grand views across the canal and architecture by Palladio.

DISTANCE: 3km (2 miles)
TIME: 2 hours
START: San Zaccaria vaporetto
END: Giudecca–Palanca vaporetto
POINTS TO NOTE: This route is especially pleasant if walked from late afternoon to early evening, in order to see the sunset across the Giudecca canal. Just be sure to time it so that you will still be able to see the interiors of the churches.

San Giorgio is the closest of the lagoon islands to the city, and the only major island untouched by commerce. Seen from afar, the majestic monastery appears suspended in the inner lagoon, with its cool Palladian church matched by a bell tower modelled on that of San Marco. Together with the Baroque beacon of La Salute, these two great symbols guard the inner harbour of Venice.

Giudecca, just off Dorsoduro, is also celebrated for its Palladian church, while Elton John's Gothic home is a more recent addition to the list of landmarks. Locals credit the rock star with turning the tide in this old working-class district, which is undergoing a widespread restoration programme.

SAN GIORGIO MAGGIORE

From the **San Zaccaria** ❶ ferry stop near San Marco, it is just a short jaunt on a No. 2 vaporetto (going clockwise) to San Giorgio Maggiore. The island was given to the Benedictines in the 10th century, and their monastery was one of the most important in the city. Seen from San Marco, the island sits stage-like in the inner lagoon, set off by its soaring campanile. The vaporetto deposits you directly in front of the church, with its Palladian facade modelled on the Classical style of ancient Rome.

Started by Palladio in 1566, and finished after his death in 1610, **San Giorgio Maggiore** ❷ (May–Sept Mon–Sat 9.30am–6.30pm, Sun 8.30–11am, 2.30–6.30pm, Oct–Apr until 5.30pm; church free, charge for bell tower) is cool, spacious and perfectly proportioned. It is also home to powerful works by Tintoretto: *The Last Supper and Gathering*

Gondolier looking out to San Giorgio

of the Manna, both executed when he was almost 80. In the Cappella dei Morti (Chapel of the Dead, often inaccessible) his Deposition (1592–4) may have been his very last work. For one of the most impressive panoramas in Venice, ask a monk to accompany you in a lift to the top of the tower. The view is even more spectacular than that from Piazza San Marco's Campanile across the water.

FONDAZIONE CINI

Coming out of the church, turn right out of the *campo* and follow the unmarked *fondamenta* until you reach Palladio's monastery, now the **Fondazione Cini** ❸ (www.cini.it; tours Sat–Sun 10am and 4pm; charge). Benedictine monks occupied the original monastery, established here at the end of the 10th century, but rebuilt after destruction by an earthquake in 1223. After the fall of the Republic the monastery was suppressed

and the complex declined over many years. Bought in 1951 by Count Vittorio Cini, it regained its role as a thriving centre of culture, becoming the base of the Fondazione Giorgio Cini. The foundation studies Venetian civilisation, and hosts contemporary exhibitions, concerts and events. The magnificent monastic complex includes the cross-vaulted refectory, Longhena's library and the Palladian Cloister of the Cypresses that leads to the monastic gardens and the Teatro Verde open-air theatre, which provides an atmospheric setting for occasional summer concerts. The new Stanze del Vetro (www.lestanzedelvetro.it) in the west wing are devoted to exhibitions, conferences and workshops on 20th-century and contemporary glass.

THE GIUDECCA

Pick up a second No. 2 vaporetto heading westwards – they go about every 10

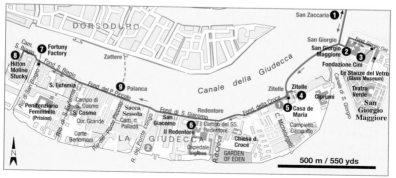

San Giorgio interior

The view from the San Giorgio bell tower

minutes. The boat makes three stops on the island on La Giudecca. This is Venice's most diverse neighbourhood: working-class pockets interspersed with palatial hotels, factories converted into funky designer flats, and monasteries converted into crafts centres.

Opinions differ as to the origins of the name Giudecca, but the most likely theory is that it derives from '*guidicati*', or judged, dating from when troublesome nobles were banished here. In the days of the Republic the island was a pleasure ground of palaces and gardens.

The Zitelle

Disembark at the first stop, Zitelle, in front of the church of the same name. The **Zitelle** ❹ (Sun at 10am for Mass only) was designed by Palladio, though completed after his death. The adjoining buildings, which now form the Bauer Palladio hotel, originally provided shelter for young women without a dowry (*zitelle* means spinsters) and taught them lace-making. Behind the Zitelle, at the tip of the island, is the deluxe Hotel Cipriani (see page 105), normally accessed by private boat.

Casa de Maria

Just right of the church is the most innovative building on the Giudecca, the **Casa de Maria** ❺, also known as the Casa dei Tre Oci (House of Three Eyes). Built from 1910 to 1913, this elaborate building was named after its architect, a Bolognese painter and photographer called Mario de Maria. The patterned brickwork facade is reminiscent of the Palazzo Ducale, while the three luminous windows are a modern hybrid of traditional Venetian Gothic architecture. The house is now the Tre Oci Cultural Centre (www.fondazionedivenezia.org, 10am–6pm daily during exhibitions only) devoted mainly to photography exhibitions and workshops. Continue west down the Fondamenta to the welcoming **I Figli delle Stelle**, see ❶.

Feast of the Redeemer

La Festa del Redentore, held on the third Sunday of July, is the most touching and intimate of Venetian festivals. It focuses on Il Redentore, the Palladian church built as a token of thanks after salvation from the plague of 1576. Venetians wend their way to the church carrying candles and reciting the rosary. A sweeping bridge of boats stretches across the Giudecca canal to the church, enabling people to attend Mass and listen to the chanting monks. The firework display on the eve of the feast day has been a feature since the 16th century. At night, crowds line the Zattere and the Giudecca or take to boats of every description, many decorated to create a fabulous night spectacle. Foghorns are sounded and fireworks blaze over the lagoon.

Il Redentore comes alive during the Feast of the Redeemer

Il Redentore

A small bridge on the Fondamenta leads to the Campo del Santissimo Redentore and one of Venice's most conspicuous landmarks. Palladio's **Il Redentore 6** (Mon–Sat 10am–5pm; Chorus Church; charge) was built to commemorate the deliverance of Venice from the 1576 plague, which took 50,000 lives – a third of the city's population. The church is the scene of Venice's most beguiling festival (see page 63). The main works of art, by Paolo Veronese and Alvise Vivarini, are in the sacristy to the right of the choir.

Continue westwards, maybe making a detour to Giudecca's boatyard, the Cantiere Crea, home to a gondola workshop, a marina and a new Venetian crafts centre, Arti Veneziane alla Giudecca, as well as housing the inn, **Al Storico da Crea**, see ❷. To get there, turn inland down the first narrow *sottoportego* after Calle San Giacomo and walk through the boatyard. The crafts centre showcases ancient skills, with master-craftsmen demonstrating mask-making and gondola-building, as well as selling Murano glass and Burano lace.

Molino Stucky

Keep heading west, crossing Ponte Longo, and looking out for the boat-lined canal and the artificial island of **Sacca Sessola** beyond. Around the Palanca waterfront is a cluster of bars, of which **Alla Palanca** is the best.

After another bridge, you will come to No. 805, the **Fortuny Factory 7** (Mon–Fri 9am–12.30pm, 2–5pm), which has been producing Fortuny fabrics since 1922. Next door is the neo-Gothic **Molino Stucky 8**, built in 1895 as a grain silo and flour mill by Giovanni Stucky, a Swiss entrepreneur who was murdered by one of his workers. The mill ceased functioning in 1954, and opened as a luxury Hilton hotel (see page 105) in 2007.

From here, backtrack to the **Palanca landing 9** and take No. 2 vaporetto back to the main island.

Food and Drink

❶ I FIGLI DELLE STELLE

Giudecca 70/71, Fondamenta delle Zitelle; tel: 041-523 0004; Thur–Tue 12.30-2.30pm, 7–10pm; closed mid-winter; €€

Sleekly decorated and with spectacular views across the Giudecca canal, this romantic restaurant combines creative cuisine with healthy dishes from Puglia, where the chef comes from.

❷ RISTORANTE AL STORICO CREA

Giudecca 212, Cantiere Nautica; tel: 041-296 0373; www.alstoricoristorante.com; closed Mon; €€

Perched above the boatyard and founded by a champion gondolier and gondola-maker, this timeless spot serves Venetian fish, game and vegetable dishes along with lagoon views.

Tintoretto's The Assumption of the Virgin, Scuola di San Rocco

SAN POLO AND SANTA CROCE

Stroll through the quiet adjoining neighbourhoods of San Polo and Santa Croce, curved into the left bank of the Grand Canal. Here, a warren of alleys and homely squares hides the great treasures of Bellini, Titian and Tintoretto in the Frari and Scuola di San Rocco.

DISTANCE: 2.5km (1.5 miles)
TIME: 3–4 hours
START/END: San Tomà vaporetto
POINTS TO NOTE: As these neighbourhoods are relatively quiet, this route is great at the weekend, when other people make a beeline for Piazza San Marco. It can be linked with The Rialto (see page 70) or Dorsoduro (see page 57) by doing it in reverse and heading south into Campo Santa Margherita after the Scuola di San Rocco.

San Polo and Santa Croce encompass the bustling Rialto market and the picturesque backwaters towards the station, centred on the quintessential campo of San Giacomo dell' Orio.

SCUOLA DI SAN ROCCO

This circular tour begins and ends at the **San Tomà vaporetto** landing stage ❶. Heading north from here, take the second right into the small Campo San Tomà. On the far side of the square you will see the former Scuola dei Calegheri; once the shoemakers' and cobblers'confraternity, it is now used as a public library. Follow the signs for the Scuola di San Rocco, one of the greatest city sights.

The **Scuola Grande di San Rocco** ❷ (Salizzada San Rocco; www.scuola grandesanrocco.it; daily 9.30am–5.30pm; charge) is the grandest of the *scuole*, or charitable lay fraternities, and acts as a backdrop for Baroque recitals. The society is dedicated to St Roch, the French saint of plague victims, who so impressed the Venetians that they stole his relics and canonised him.

The 16th-century building is also a shrine to Tintoretto. He was one of several eminent contenders for the decoration of the Scuola, Veronese among them, but caught his competitors unawares by producing a completed painting, rather than the requested cartoon. He worked on the Scuola on and off for 24 years, producing powerful biblical scenes. The series of paintings reveals Tintoretto's revolutionary ability to con-

The Frari is the largest of all the Venetian Gothic churches

vey theatrical effect through contrasts of light and shade, bold foreshortening, visionary effects of colour and unusual viewpoints.

In the lower hall the paintings illustrate scenes from the *Life of the Virgin*, while the upper hall has paintings over 4.8m (16ft) high, depicting scenes from the *Life of Christ* and, on the ceiling, images from the Old Testament. Use the mirrors provided to view the ceiling without straining your neck.

At the far end of the Sala dell' Albergo, scenes from *The Passion* culminate in *The Crucifixion* itself, fittingly the largest, most moving and dramatic painting of the collection. *The Glorification of St Roch* on the ceiling of the same room was the work that won Tintoretto the commission.

THE FRARI CHURCH

Retrace your steps to the Salizzada San Rocco, stopping for a pick-me-up *gelato* at **Millevoglie**, see ❶. From here you can see the apse end of the **Frari Church ❸** (Campo dei Frari; Mon–Sat 9am–5.30pm, Sun 1–5.30pm; www.basilicadei frari.it; Chorus Church, see page 125; charge), which abuts Campo San Rocco. Follow the side of the church around, taking in its simple Gothic brick facade before entering.

Along with the church of Santi Giovanni e Paolo (see page 53) in Castello, the Frari is the finest Gothic church in Venice. It is also the resting place of the great master of Venetian painting, Titian, and home to two of his very finest works of art. The hulking bare-brick building and adjoining monastic cloisters were built in the 14th and 15th centuries by Franciscan friars, whose first principle was poverty – hence the meagre decoration of the facade. The soaring bell tower is the tallest in Venice, after the campanile in Piazza San Marco (see page 30).

The interior

Inside, the eye is drawn to Titian's rich *Assumption of the Virgin*, which crowns the main altar. On the left side of the church the same artist's *Madonna di Ca' Pesaro* is another masterpiece of light, colour and harmony, and one of the earliest works to show the Madonna out of the centre of the composition. Members of the Pesaro family, who commissioned the work, can be seen in the lower half of the painting. Directly opposite is Titian's mausoleum, erected 300 years after his death.

Other outstanding works of art here include Giovanni Bellini's beautiful *Madonna* and *Child with Saints* in the sacristy; the finely carved 15th-century monks' choir; the wooden statue by Donatello of St John the Baptist on the altarpiece to the right of the main altar; and the rather sinister monument to Canova (located to the left of the side door).

A beautiful morning on Calle dei Spezier, Santa Croce

SCUOLA DI SAN GIOVANNI EVANGELISTA

Back in Campo dei Frari, cross the bridge out of the square and turn left onto Fondamenta dei Frari. Cross another bridge, turn left, and then right onto Calle del Magazen and the **Scuola di San Giovanni Evangelista ❹**. The church is part of a labyrinthine quarter of narrow alleys (*calli*) and covered passageways (*sottoporteghi*). Though the Scuola is only open by appointment (www.scuolasangiovanni.it), the exterior courtyard is lovely, while the theatrical interior can be seen by anyone attending an opera at the confraternity house. Established in 1261, the Scuola was one of the six major confraternities, largely due to its ownership of a piece of the True Cross, and played a leading role in the ceremonial life of the city.

SANTA CROCE

Exiting the courtyard, turn left and stroll down the street, soaking up the local flavour in this quiet section of town. A little way along, look out for a small courtyard on the right with a terracotta pavement laid in a herringbone pattern. At one time, most of Venice's streets were paved in this fashion. At the end of the street, turn left and cross the bridge over the canal, entering into **Campiello del Cristo**.

We are now in the *sestiere* of Santa Croce. Though centrally located, this district is bypassed by the majority of tourists, probably because of its lack of 'big name' sites. But thankfully this

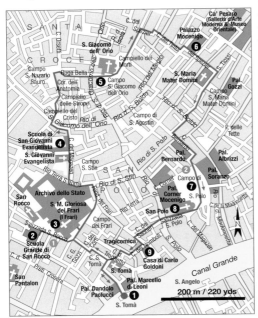

Palazzo Mocenigo's red drawing room

affords the opportunity to enjoy a slice of real Venetian life. The bridge offers a nice view of an enclosed garden with large trees, evidence that many homes do have gardens, even in Venice.

Go straight through the *campiello*, continuing to Campo San Nazario Sauro. Heading east out of the square via the Ruga Bella brings you to the **Campo San Giacomo dell'Orio** ❺. Here you will find Venetians young and old gathering to chat in the cafés, gossip on the red benches or shop at the small grocery. Take the time to relax, maybe join local people for a drink at **Al Prosecco**, see page 112, or have a meal at **Il Refolo**, see page 114.

PALAZZO MOCENIGO

The tour now begins to loop back to San Polo. Exit from Campo San Giacomo dell'Orio via the road that runs next to Al Prosecco. Follow the signs to the vaporetto and you will soon reach **Palazzo Mocenigo** ❻ (Salizzada San Stae 1992; www.mocenigo.visitmuve.it; Tue–Sun 10am–5pm, until 4pm in winter; charge) not to be confused with the Palazzo Mocenigo on the Grand Canal. The ancestral residence of one of the greatest dogal families it is now now home to an eclectic collection of period costume, ranging from corsets to knee-breeches, mainly from the 18th and 19th centuries. It is also a great chance to view a 17th-century palatial mansion, with its opulent furnishings intact,

and the portrait gallery of a dynasty that produced seven doges.

CAMPO SAN POLO

Leaving the *palazzo*, take a left and continue along the street that led you here, cross over two bridges, then turn right into Campo Santa Maria Mater Domini. Cross the *campo*, taking the street as far as you can before turning left onto Rio Terà Bernardo. Following the street south will lead you directly into **Campo di San Polo** ❼, the largest square in Venice after Piazza San Marco. Once the site of bull-baiting, tournaments, masked balls and fairs, it is now the scene of less festive activities such as football and cycling. You might decide to have lunch on the square at this point, at **Antica Birraria la Corte**, see ❷; this is also a good late-night option, if you'd prefer to come back another time.

Highlights

The church of **San Polo** ❽ (Mon–Sat 10am–5pm; Chorus Church, see page 125; charge) is worth a visit for the cycle of the *Stations of the Cross* painted by Tiepolo when he was only 20 years old (follow the sign for the Crucis del Tiepolo) and Tintoretto's *Last Supper*. The foot of the church's nearby campanile is embellished with two Romanesque lions, one playing with a serpent, the other with a human head.

Next to the church, the classical **Palazzo Corner-Mocenigo** was for a

Statue of Carlo Goldoni

while the residence of Frederick Rolfe (self-styled Baron Corvo), a notoriously eccentric English writer. It was here that he wrote *The Desire and Pursuit of the Whole*, ruthlessly lampooning English society in Venice. As a result his host threw him out, penniless, onto the streets. On the opposite side of the square is the **Palazzo Soranzo** with its sweeping pink Gothic facade. Casanova came to the palace as a young, hired violinist, living as the adopted son and heir to the family fortune with access to Venetian society. From here he went on to seduce and outrage Europe's 18th-century aristocracy.

MASK SHOPS

Turn right out of the church and cross the bridge. Along **Calle dei Saoneri** and the streets beyond, sequined mask and souvenir shops have replaced some of the Venetian craft shops, but it's still fun for browsing, and the occasional artisan can be spotted creating glass insects, fashioning a traditional leather mask or making marble-effect paper. At the end of Calle dei Saoneri, turn left, then right into Calle dei Nomboli. Halfway along, the stunning masks in the window of **Tragicomica** (No. 2800, www.tragicomica.it) are handmade by craftsmen – hence the prices. Masks range from *commedia dell'arte* characters (see page 21) to allegorical masks of the creator's own invention, as well as hand-sewn *commedia dell'arte Carnival* costumes for hire or sale.

CASA GOLDONI

Opposite the shop is **Casa Goldoni** ❾ (Calle dei Nomboli 2794; www.casagoldoni.visitmuve.it.it; Thur–Tue Apr–Oct 10am–5pm, Nov–Mar 10am–4pm; charge), birthplace of the 18th-century dramatist. Goldoni's plays are famed for their wit, and for his espousal of *commedia dell'arte*, creating a new genre called *opera buffa* (comic opera). Like other private residences or confraternity houses in the area, the Casa is often used for concerts. From here, follow signs for the vaporetto back to San Tomà.

Food and Drink

❶ GELATERIA MILLEVOGLIE

San Polo 3033; Salizzada San Rocco; tel: 041-524 4667; daily until late; €
Reputedly the area's best ice-cream parlour. Try the fig and tiramisu flavours.

❷ ANTICA BIRRARIA LA CORTE

San Polo 2168, Campo San Polo; tel: 041-275 0570; closed Mon; €
This former brewery represents good value, and offers ample outdoor and indoor seating, which makes it a popular option for large groups. Inventive salads, home-made pasta, pizzas, and beer, of course. No credit cards.

The Rialto Bridge at night

THE RIALTO

To Venetians, the Rialto is not restricted to the graceful bridge, but embraces the district curved around the middle bend of the Grand Canal – a labyrinth of dark alleys and tiny squares centred on its quayside markets.

DISTANCE: 1.5km (1 mile)

TIME: 2 hours

START: Rialto Mercato vaporetto

END: Taverna Campiello del Remer (on the opposite bank)

POINTS TO NOTE: Make an early start to see the markets in full swing and watch the barges offloading at the quayside by the Grand Canal. The best days to do this tour are Tuesday to Saturday, when both main markets are functioning. The Rialto market marks the start of a Venetian bar crawl, a *giro di ombre*, in the backstreet wine and tapas bars known as *bacari*. Expect an array of exotic Venetian snacks (*cicchetti*) and glasses of wine (*ombre*) in snug, rough-and-ready bars, often dating back to the 15th century. Traditional Rialto bars close early so either go for lunch or for an early supper.

It was in the Rialto – for centuries the commercial hub of the city – that the first inhabitants of the lagoon are said to have settled. By the heyday of the Republic it was one of the major financial quarters of Europe – a thriving centre for bankers, brokers and merchants. The quarter is only a shadow of its former self, but it remains a hive of commercial activity with locals purchasing fresh produce and hawkers catching the tourists as they cross the famous bridge.

RIALTO MARKETS

Set off from the **Rialto Mercato vaporetto ❶** and walk straight ahead into Campo Bella Vienna, a bustling square that is home to Il Muro, an inviting *bacaro*, (see page 41).

Turn right onto the Casaria, lined with market stalls and butchers' shops, which will deliver you into the heart of the **Erberia ❷**, a fruit-and-vegetable market.

The market extends along the canal banks to the **Pescheria ❸**, the fish market in an arcaded neo-Gothic hall by the quayside. Much of the fish is brought in from Chioggia, a fishing town on a small island on the southern edge of the lagoon.

The neo Gothic Pescheria   *Rialto fishmonger*

Turn left down Calle Beccarie into Campo delle Beccarie, and, if the mood takes you, join fishmongers at nearby **Do Mori**, see ❶, or one of the other Rialto *bacari*.

BEYOND THE RIALTO

Leave the Campo via the little bridge in the corner and follow the yellow sign for Ca' Pesaro under the *sottoportego*. Turn left onto Calle dei Botteri and follow the street until it narrows, and turn right into the little square marked Carampane. Pass under the *sottoportego*, then take a right into Rio Terà delle Carampane. The bridge on your right is the **Ponte delle Tette** ❹ (Bridge of Breasts), named after the prostitutes (there were some 11,000 in 16th-century Venice) who frequented this quarter, stripping to the waist to entice customers.

Return to the Rio Terà delle Carampane, where you'll find **Antiche Carampane** (see page 113).

SAN SILVESTRO

After lunch, take a right into the narrow Calle Albrizzi for Campiello Abrizzo then follow Calle Tamossi left off the square until you reach a canal. Cross the bridge on your left, passing the Al Ponte Storto, an *osteria* that may tempt you, if lunch is

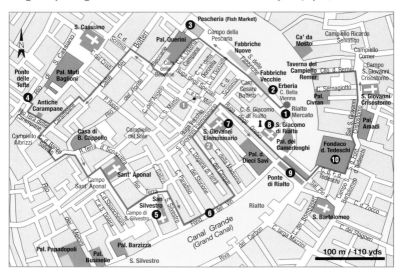

Rialto Bridge relief

still on the cards. Follow Calle del Ponte Storto into Campo Sant'Aponal. This square may be tiny, but with eight streets leading into it, it is a crowded crossroads. The deconsecrated church of Sant'Aponal is used as an archive. Cross the Campo and head south under the *sottoportego*, turning left for Campo di San Silvestro.

Originally founded in the 12th century, the church of **San Silvestro** ❺ (daily 8–11.30am, 3.30–6.30pm but closed indefinitely for restoration) was completely rebuilt during the 19th century (the facade was completed in 1909). The highlight of the neoclassical interior is Tintoretto's *Baptism of Christ* (first altar on the right).

Pass in front of the church and turn right along Rio Terrà San Silvestro, which leads back to the Grand Canal. Turn left onto the **Fondamenta del Vin** ❻, where barrels of wine used to be unloaded. It is overrun by souvenir stalls and touristy restaurants, but don't be drawn in by the beseeching waiters. Instead, stroll a short way along the canal until you come to the Sottoportego e Calle dei Cinque, where coffee connoisseurs should stop for a treat at **Caffè del Doge**, see ❷.

SAN GIOVANNI AND SAN GIACOMO

Continue up Calle dei Cinque, and turn right into San Giovanni Elemosinario, lined with souvenir stalls and teeming with people making their way to the Rialto Bridge. Tucked away behind a metal gate on your right, the church of **San Giovanni Elemosinario** ❼ (Mon–Sat 10am–5pm; Chorus Church, see page 125; charge) is one of the oldest churches in the area. Pop in here to see Titian's altarpiece *San Giovanni Elemosinario*, a touching portrayal of the saint giving alms; it is characterised by the loose brush strokes that would mark the artist's later works.

Turn right outside the church, then right again onto Ruga degli Orefici, passing the oldest church in the area, **San Giacomo di Rialto** ❽. Nestling comfortably among the fruit-and-vegetable stalls, the church is linked to St James, patron saint of goldsmiths and pilgrims. Both were much in evidence in the Rialto. Its most distinctive features are the Gothic portico, bell tower and bold 24-hour clock.

Campo San Giacomo preserves its mercantile atmosphere, an echo of Republican times, when money-changers and bankers set up their tables under the church portico, and in the neighbouring **Bancogiro**, now a wine bar. The **Gobbo di Rialto** (Hunchback of the Rialto) is a curious stooped figure supporting the steps opposite the church: it was on the adjoining podium that republican laws were proclaimed, with the burden borne metaphorically by this figure of the Venetian Everyman.

RIALTO BRIDGE

Spanning the Grand Canal is the marble **Ponte di Rialto** ❾, a single-span

San Giacomo di Rialto clock

The graceful bridge

bridge lined with shops. Until the 1850s, it was the only fixed point for crossing the canal. The current structure is actually the fourth version of the bridge. The first wooden structure was erected in the 14th century, only to be destroyed during a revolt in 1310. A second structure collapsed under the weight of spectators who had gathered to watch the procession for the Marquis of Ferrara in 1444. One can see what the third version looked like by viewing Carpaccio's *Miracle of the True Cross* in the Accademia (see page 42). The current bridge was designed by the appropriately named Antonio da Ponte at the end of the 16th century. The relatively unknown architect won the commission over giants such as Michelangelo, Sansovino and Palladio.

Today the bridge is tightly packed with shops and stalls selling trinkets, leather, jewellery and silk. Walk along the side aisles, if possible, as they tend to be less crowded than the centre, and the balustrades make a wonderful vantage point over the palaces, warehouses and water traffic along the busiest stretch of the Grand Canal.

THE RIGHT BANK

The building across the bridge to the left is the **Fondaco dei Tedeschi** ❿, named after the German merchants who leased the emporium. It is swathed in scaffolding while it undergoes restoration by Benetton who bought the palace (see page 38). Turn left around the back of the

building (away from the San Marco sign) and cross the bridge into Campo San Giovanni Cristostomo. For a truly Venetian experience, take the alley on the left, next to the Fiaschetteria Toscana and follow the street under the *sottoportego* for the **Taverna del Campiello Remer** (see page 115).

(see page 115).

> ## Food and Drink
>
> **① DO MORI**
> San Polo 429; Calle Do Mori; tel: 041-522 5401; Mon–Sat; €
> This ancient inn is the most picturesque of *bacari*, with a cosy atmosphere. Service is slightly brusque, and the Prosecco not the finest, but the *cicchetti* are reliable and include *francobolli* (literally postage stamps), tiny treats of traditional tapas, from slivers of dried salt cod to meatballs or sweet and sour sardines. To find Do Mori, take Ruga degli Speziali off to the left as you come into Campo delle Beccarie, then take the third turning on the left.
>
> **② CAFFÈ DEL DOGE**
> San Polo 609; Calle dei Cinque; tel: 041-522 7787; www.caffedeldoge.com; Mon–Sat 7am–7pm, Sun 7am–1pm; €
> Sniff out the best coffee in Venice at a bustling coffee house where they roast their own Arabica beans. Venetian celebrity chef Enrica Rocca also recommends the Giacometto, 'coffee blended with hazelnut chocolate, cream and toasted almonds'.

Campo del Ghetto Nuovo

CANNAREGIO

Largely residential, Cannaregio is one of the most fascinating but least explored areas of the city. On this half-day route you visit the world's oldest Ghetto, the peaceful backwaters of the Madonna dell'Orto neighbourhood, and some of the finest Gothic and Renaissance churches in Venice.

DISTANCE: 3km (2 miles)
TIME: 3–4 hours
START: Stazione Ferroviaria
END: Santa Maria dei Miracoli
POINTS TO NOTE: In summer, this route is best walked early in the morning or late in the afternoon to escape the heat. You might also want to avoid Saturdays, as it's the Sabbath, and most of the Ghetto is closed. The route can easily be combined with No. 5 (done in reverse) via a short walk to Campo SS Giovanni e Paolo.

Cannaregio is the second-largest district in Venice (Castello is the biggest) and the most densely populated, with about 20,000 residents. Glimpses of everyday life on secluded balconies or through half-shuttered blinds reveal elderly Venetians passing the time of day with their neighbours, or leaning out of windows hung with washing. The tangle of alleys reveals the occasional *bottega* selling woodcarvings, as well as hole-in-the-wall bars and small *alimentari* (grocery stores), a rarity in more up-market parts of Venice.

LISTA DI SPAGNA

Start at the **Stazione Ferroviaria S. Lucia ①** (Train Station) and follow the flow along the Lista di Spagna, then take the Ponte delle Guglie (Bridge of the Obelisks) across the Cannaregio Canal. This waterway was the main entrance to the city before the railway bridge was built in 1846 to link the city to the mainland. This is a lively quarter with waterside stalls and a morning market along the Rio Terrà San Leonardo ahead of you.

THE GHETTO

Turn left after the bridge where you see a yellow sign in Hebrew and Italian directing you to the Synagogue, and take the third covered passage on the right signposted 'Sinagoghe'. Before continuing, you might consider a Kosher bite to eat at **Gam-Gam**, see **①**.

Holocaust memorial in the Ghetto Nuovo

This passageway, dotted with small shops, galleries and workshops, leads to the **Ghetto Vecchio** (Old Ghetto) and Campiello delle Scuole. Cross the bridge into the **Campo del Ghetto Nuovo** (New Ghetto Square), which, despite the name, stands at the heart of world's oldest ghetto, a fortified island created in 1516. The site was formerly an iron foundry or *ghetto* in Venetian and the word gave its name to Jewish and other segregated quarters all over the world.

In the early 16th century, Jews in Venice were confined to this tiny section of Cannaregio, surrounded on all sides by canals. It became one of the major Jewish communities in Europe with a population density three times greater than in the most crowded Christian suburb. The only answer to these cramped conditions was to build upwards. Hence the 'skyscrapers' of Venice, tenement blocks of five or six storeys that were once the highest in Europe. The Jews were heavily taxed, barred from many professions and forced to observe a strict curfew. The community remained on the site until 1797, when Napoleon had the gates torn down, and from then on Jews had the freedom to live wherever they liked in the city. Today, only a handful of Jewish families live here, but the area is rich in Jewish culture, with restaurants, bakeries, B&Bs and Jewish handicrafts that serve the 500-strong Jewish community in Venice.

Jewish Museum

The **Museo Ebraico** ❷ (Campo del Ghetto Nuovo 2902/b; www.museo ebraico.it; Sun–Fri June–Sept 10am–7pm, Oct–May 10am–5.30pm except Jewish holidays; charge) is to be found on the opposite side of the square. From here English and Italian guided tours of the Spanish, German and Levantine synagogues take place from 10.30am–5.30pm, off season to 4.30pm (charge).

Fondamenta degli Ormesini

Take the northern exit from the square, cross the bridge with wrought-iron railings and turn right into the **Fondamenta degli Ormesini**. The bustling quaysides and neighbourhood mood may also help explain why Cannaregio has such good *bacari*. With its affordable prices and picturesque canalside setting, **Al Timon**, see ❷, may tempt you to take a break for a glass of wine and light meal.

TINTORETTO'S NEIGHBOURHOOD

Turn left down the narrow Calle del Forno, cross the bridge and turn right into the pretty Fondamenta della Sensa. Follow the canal as far as **Campo dei Mori**, home to **L'Orto dei Mori**, see ❸. The statues here depict merchants of the Mastelli family, who came to Venice from the Peloponnese in the 12th century.

Merchant statue, Campo dei Mori

Tintoretto's House

Beyond the Campo, another turbaned merchant occupies a niche in the wall, just before the **Casa di Tintoretto** ❸ (Fondamenta dei Mori 3399). The nondescript building is marked with a plaque and bas-relief of the artist, who lived here with his family from 1574 until his death in 1594. Jacopo Robusti derived his nickname, Tintoretto, from his father's profession of dyer *(tintore)*. He spent his whole life in Cannaregio and only left Venice once.

Towards Madonna dell'Orto

Return to the Campo dei Mori, cross the bridge on the far side and turn right for views of the relief of a one-legged man and a camel on the canal

facade of the Gothic **Palazzo Mastelli**, which adds to the Eastern flavour of this area.

Nearby is the **Madonna dell'Orto** ❹ (Campo della Madonna dell'Orto; Mon–Sat 10am–5pm; Chorus Church, see page 125; charge), a masterpiece of Venetian Gothic, conspicuous for its oriental campanile, richly embellished facade and beautiful carved portal. This was Tintoretto's beloved parish church and it is decorated with works he created *in situ* – arguably his finest outside the Scuola di San Rocco (see page 65). The artist is buried in the chapel to the right of the altar.

In the north aisle of you might notice an empty sculpted frame. This held Giovanni Bellini's Madonna, which was sto-

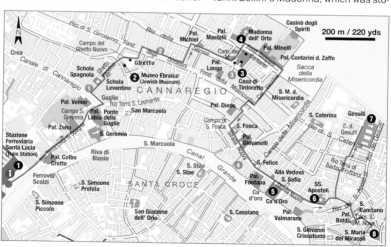

Ca d'Oro

Santa Maria dei Miracoli

len in 1993. The frame has remained empty ever since.

CA' D'ORO

Follow the canal eastwards, crossing the bridge at the end. From here you can catch glimpses across the lagoon of the islands of San Michele and Murano. Continue to the end of the street, crossing over three bridges, until you rejoin the throng in Campo di Santa Fosca. Follow Strada Nova eastwards to the Ca' d'Oro, catching your breath in a quirky Cannaregio *bacaro* such as **La Cantina**, see ❹, or **Alla Vedova** (see page 115).

The **Ca' d'Oro** ❺, one of the finest palaces on the Grand Canal, is home to the **Franchetti Gallery** (Calle Ca' d'Oro 3932; www.cadoro.org; Mon 8.15am–2pm, Tue–Sun 8.15am–7.15pm; charge), a collection of Renaissance treasures. The most prized piece is Mantegna's *St Sebastian*; Tullio Lombardo's delightful marble *Double Portrait*, inspired by ancient funerary reliefs, is also worth singling out. The *portego* is a showcase of sculpture and opens onto the Grand Canal. The palace interior suffered barbaric restoration in the mid-19th century, but still offers fantastic views of the Grand Canal.

Coming out of the Ca' d'Oro, turn right back onto the Strada Nova for the bustling *campo* and church of **SS Apostoli** ❻ (8am–noon, 5–7pm), which houses a painting by Tiepolo.

THE GESUITI

Take the northern exit out of the *campo*, behind the church, and you'll come to a small square. At the end of Calle del Manganer, take a left, crossing two bridges until you reach the **Campo dei Gesuiti**. The large ex-monastery of the Jesuits on your right, with bricked-up windows, was once used as a barracks and is awaiting restoration.

San Michele

San Michele, site of the city cemetery, is easily identified from the mainland by its solemn cypress trees. As the island closest to Venice, it is served by ferries from the Fondamente Nuove. Formerly a prison island, it was Napoleon who decreed that the dead should be brought here, away from the crowded city. The rambling cemetery is lined with gardens stacked with simple memorials or domed family mausoleums. Here lie the tombs of dogal families, obscure diplomats and plague victims, along with such illustrious figures as Stravinsky, Ezra Pound and Diaghilev. Famous foreigners are allowed to rest in peace, but more modest souls tend to be evicted – after 10 years their remains are exhumed and placed in permanent storage boxes. By the landing stage, the cemetery's focal point is the Renaissance church of San Michele in Isola. A trip to this peaceful and remote spot is haunting and memorable.

Intricate ceiling detail in Santa Maria dei Miracoli

A little further along is the **Gesuiti** ❼ (10am–noon, 4–6pm), an extravagant Jesuit church founded in 1714: the interior is a riot of gilded stucco and sculpted green-and-white marble, masquerading as drapery. Titian's *Martyrdom of St Lawrence* hangs above the altar on the left.

Just north of the church are fine lagoon views from the Fondamente Nuove. Depending on the light, these northern quays can look bleak and washed out or moodily magnificent. If time allows, consider a trip to the cemetery island of San Michele (see box) by taking the 41 or 42 vaporetto towards Murano for one stop.

SANTA MARIA DEI MIRACOLI

For your final destination, head out of Campo dei Gesuiti the way you came in, walk as far as Calle Muazzo, then follow the signs for Ospedale SS Giovanni e Paolo and Santa Maria dei Miracoli through Campo S. Canzian until you reach Campo S. Maria.

Across the bridge and to the right is the ornate Renaissance church of **Santa Maria dei Miracoli** ❽ (Campo Santa Maria dei Miracoli; Mon–Sat 10am–5pm; Chorus Church, see page 125; charge). Rising sheer from the water, the facade offers a dazzling display of marble. Inside, the surfaces are a vision of pale pinks and silvery greys, and pilasters adorned with interlaced flowers, mythical creatures and cavorting mermaids. Not surprisingly this Renaissance gem is a favourite with Venetian brides.

Food and Drink

❶ GAM-GAM

Cannaregio 1122, Ponte delle Guglie; tel: 041-275 9256; www.gamgamkosher.com; Sun–Thur noon–10pm, Fri 12pm–two hours before sunset, Sat one hour after sunset–11pm; €€
The Kosher Gam-Gam is a focal point for the Jewish community and serves Italian, Israeli and vaguely Middle Eastern dishes.

❷ AL TIMON

Cannaregio 2754, Fondamenta degli Ormesini (Guglie ferry stop); tel: 041-524 6066; Tue–Sun; €
A beautiful canalside setting and laid-back atmosphere make this a favourite. Does three or four hot dishes a day, plus salads and delicious *crostini*.

❸ L'ORTO DEI MORI

Cannaregio 3386, Campo dei Mori; tel: 041 524 3677; www.osteriaortodeimori.com; closed Tue; €€
This little *osteria* in an irresistible setting on Campo dei Mori does Venetian classics and great seafood pasta.

❹ LA CANTINA

Cannaregio 3689, Campo San Felice; tel: 041-522 8258; Tue–Sat; €€
In this simple *bacaro*, feasts of charcuterie, cheeses, carpaccio, seafood platters, soups and bruschetta are matched by fine wines. Slow service.

Venetian glass

MURANO, BURANO AND TORCELLO

Spend a day exploring this trio of lagoon islands. Watch glass-blowing in Murano, wander the canal banks of psychedelic Burano, the friendliest island, and be stirred by Torcello, once the principal settlement of Venice.

DISTANCE: 5km (3.25 miles)
TIME: A full day
START: Museo vaporetto, Murano
END: Museo di Torcello, Torcello
POINTS TO NOTE: Buy a vaporetto pass, as you will need to use several different boats. To reach the starting point, take vaporetto 4.1 or 4.2 from Fondamente Nuove or San Zaccaria (both also stop at San Michele) or No. 3 from Piazzale Roma or Ferrovia. Avoid weekends, when the islands are packed. Beware of free trips offered by touts near Piazza San Marco, who are paid a hefty commission for each tourist brought to a showroom.

MURANO

The island of Murano is sometimes described as a mini-Venice. It cannot match the city for splendour but, like Venice, it is made up of islands and divided by canals, lined with mansions and *palazzi*. It even has its own Grand Canal. But Murano's *raison d'être* has

always been the making of glass. As early as the 7th century a glass industry was established near Venice. In the late 13th century the factories were moved to Murano to avoid the hazards of fire from the open furnaces.

Murano glassmakers enjoyed rare privileges, but their craft was a closely guarded secret, and the makers left the shores of Venice on pain of death. Even so, many of them were lured abroad in the 16th century. Those who were discovered, including a few who divulged their secrets to the court of Louis XIV, were condemned to death. Today over 60 percent of the glass produced here is exported. The characteristics of the local glass are deep, bright colours and ornate design.

It's easy to get to the island independently. To avoid the pressure from pushy glass vendors, wait until the **Museo stop ❶** on Murano before getting off. Signs indicate the **Museo del Vetro ❷** (Glass Museum, Fondamenta Giustinian 8; www.museovetro.visit muve.it; Thur–Tue Apr–Oct 10am–6pm, Nov–Mar 10am–5pm; charge;

A panoramic view of Murano

guided tours in English and French Tue and Thur at noon and 2.30pm), containing an eclectic collection of Venetian glass in a 15th-century palazzo. A prize piece is the Coppa Barovier (Barovier being one of a dynasty of Muranese glassmakers) – a 15th-century wedding chalice adorned with allegorical love scenes.

SS Maria e Donato

Leaving the museum, turn left and follow Fondamenta Giustinian for the basilica of **SS Maria e Donato ❸** (Campo San Donato; 9am–noon, 3.30–7pm, closed Sun am). Founded in the 7th century and remodelled in the Veneto-Byzantine style, it is the finest church on Murano. Despite heavy-handed restoration, it retains some outstanding features: the colonnaded apse with decorative brickwork on the canalside; the 12th-century mosaic *pavimento*, adorned with medieval motifs and animals; the ship's keel roof; and the apse mosaic of the *Madonna and Child*.

Fondamenta Longa

Retrace your steps to the Museo ferry stop, follow the Fondamenta Longa along Murano's own Canal Grande and cross the Ponte Vivarini (some-

times called Ponte Longo), named after a 15th-century family of painters who lived on Murano. From the bridge you can see the **Palazzo da Mula** (on the far bank to your right), one of Murano's few surviving grand mansions.

Fondamenta dei Vetrai

Across the bridge to the left is the Gothic **San Pietro Martire ❹** (Fondamenta dei Vetrai; 9am–noon, 3–6pm, closed Sun am) housing a fine altarpiece by Giovanni Bellini (on the right if you enter by the main door). The interior also contains spectacular Murano glass chandeliers and bottle-glass windows in lovely hues. If feeling hungry, cross the canal via the bridge facing

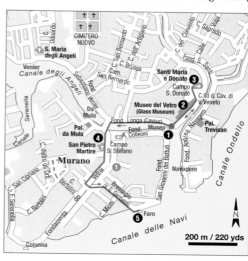

Glassblower at work in Murano.

the church into Campo Santo Stefano, and enjoy a meal at **Trattoria Busa alla Torre**, see ❶.

Afterwards, amble along the **Fondamenta dei Vetrai**, the heart of the glass-making district. The glassworks and showrooms along the quayside offer a chance to admire the glass-blowers' skills. In the morning, market boats selling fresh produce along the canal add to the busy scene. If you haven't yet seen a glass-blowing display, be lured into one of the workshops. With incredible skill the maestro blows the blob of molten glass, then with a spatula and a pair of pincers, twists, turns, pinches and flattens it into the shape of an animal or bird.

To continue to Burano, cross the canal at Ponte de Mezo and take Viale Bressagio across the square. This leads to the **Murano Faro stop ❺**, and vaporetto 12 for the 30-minute ride.

BURANO

Burano is a splash of colour in a bleak lagoon, dispelling any mournfulness with its parade of colourful fishermen's cottages and bobbing boats. Burano also makes a cheery lunch stop en route to Torcello, its polar opposite, or a dinner stop on the way back from Torcello. Naturally hospitable, the islanders are increasingly known for their 'Slow Food' inns rather than for their lacemaking and fishing traditions. The lace and linen stalls on the island vie for attention but most of these tablecloths and napkins have been factory-made in Asia. As with Murano glass, beware of imitations.

From the **landing stage ❻**, mill down via Marcello, past brightly painted houses. Turn left at the end of the street and cross over the bridge, turning left again onto the Fondamenta degli Assassini. To view the most colourful courtyard on the island, take the tiny alley marked Via al Gattolo. At No. 339, **Casa Bepi ❼** has a dazzling multicoloured, geometrical facade.

If hungry, make your way to Via Baldassare Galuppi, the main street, named after the composer who was born here. Try either the **Trattoria da Romano** (see page 117), or **Al Gatto Nero**, see ❷. Stick to fish and you will not be disappointed.

Lace and linen

Lacemaking was a traditional occupation for fishermen's wives, whose menfolk were away at sea. In the 16th century, Burano lace was in great demand, so much so that the court of Louis XIV closed its doors to Venetian lace and created a royal industry of its own. Every means possible was used to steal the industry from La Serenissima, by inducing women to leave Burano and providing them with workshops that recreated Venetian designs.

The downfall of the Republic led to the inevitable decline of the lace industry, but a revival took place in 1872

Psychedelic Burano

when a lacemaking school was founded in an effort to combat local poverty. Today, Burano is one of the last surviving centres of handmade lace, and the Buranesi struggle valiantly to keep the tradition alive.

To see authentic Burano lace and the women who make it, visit the revamped **Museo del Merletto ❽** (Lace Museum; Piazza Galuppi; www.museomerletto. visitmuve.it; Wed–Mon Apr–Oct 10am–6pm, Nov–Mar 10am–5pm ; charge). Here priceless antique pieces are displayed behind glass.

Mazzorbo

From Burano, cross the wooden footbridge to the more rural island of **Mazzorbo**. At first sight it looks similar to Burano: the same colourful cottages lining the canal. Here too, when not ruining their eyesight poring over lace, the fishermen's wives painted the family homes in psychedelic colours, often adding geometrical motifs over the doorways. But there the similarities end. You soon catch sight of a sluggish canal, a walled vineyard, and a solitary brick bell tower (14th-century).

On the waterfront lies the entrance to the lagoon's last walled vineyard, now at the heart of a model estate encompassing a cosy inn and gourmet restaurant, **Venissa** (see page 117). The vineyard has been planted with Dorona, the golden grape beloved by the doges, once widely cultivated on the lagoon but now at risk of extinction.

Food and Drink

❶ TRATTORIA BUSA ALLA TORRE
Campo Santo Stefano 3, Murano (Faro ferry stop); tel: 041-739 662; lunch only, closed Mon; €€
This classic Venetian seafood restaurant, with a spacious terrace on the piazza, has been an inn since 1420 and a wine store since the 12th century. Clams, crabs, fish grills are generally reliable, as are *sarde in saor* (marinated sardines).

❷ AL GATTO NERO
Via Giudecca 88, Burano;
tel: 041-730 120, www.gattonero.com;
Tue–Sun; €€
This long-established family-run seafood restaurant is famous for risotto alla Buranella, grilled mixed fried fish as well as for lagoon vegetables, such as Sant'Erasmo artichokes, or home-made pasta made with tiny lagoon crabs.

❸ AL PONTE DEL DIAVOLO
Fondamenta Borgognoni 10, Torcello;
tel: 041-730 401; early Feb–late Nov Tue–Sun 11am–5pm; www.osteriaalpontedel diavolo.com; €€€
This is a hospitable and atmospheric (lunch only) spot, overlooking a garden, with pasta and seafood dishes predominating.

Colourful Burano

Lace umbrellas for sale in Burano

For now, retrace your steps to the ferry and head for Torcello, a short jaunt from Burano on Line 9, which departs every half-hour and speeds across to the island in about five minutes.

TORCELLO

Torcello, the most remote of these islands (an hour by ferry), is the least populated but, for many, the most resonant. This marshy, unprepossessing spot was the site of the original settlement in the Venetian lagoon. It is hard to believe it was once the centre of a thriving civilisation. In its heyday, Torcello's population was 20,000, but this figure has fallen to a mere 50. As Venice rose to power, decline set in, trade on the island dwindled and the waters silted up. Today the cathedral, church and a couple of *palazzi* are the sole evidence of past splendour. But it is this palpable sense of loss that makes Torcello such a nostalgic spot.

From the **landing stage** ❾, where the cathedral bell tower soars above the marshland, follow the well-beaten towpath to the centre of civilisation, such as it is. If you arrive at lunchtime, enjoy a life-enhancing feast in **Locanda Cipriani** (see page 117). Hemingway, Queen Elizabeth II, Sir Winston Churchill, Charlie Chaplin and Sophia Loren are just a few who have made the same journey to this famed outpost. A less pricey alternative is the rustic **Al Ponte del Diavolo**, see ❸.

The minor islands

As your boat takes you through the northern lagoon, past Murano, and on towards Burano and Torcello, you will pass a number of small islands. On your right for most of the journey from Murano to Burano, you can see the marshy islets and main island of Sant'Erasmo, whose fruit and vegetables end up in the Rialto market. First, however, you pass Le Vignole, an island where, in summer, many Venetians stop to swim and eat at the rustic restaurant here (Alle Vignole; Apr–Sept Tue–Sun). Both Le Vignole and Sant'Erasmo are accessible by vaporetto No. 13 from the Fondamente Nuove, but the service is sporadic.

The ferry swings left around the deserted island of San Giacomo in Palude, one of many abandoned in the 1960s. To the right, in the distance, a dark cluster of cypresses marks the island of San Francesco del Deserto, where St Francis is said to have retreated in 1220. The island is not accessible by public transport, so you will need to hire a water taxi from the rank next to the vaporetto stop – or go on a boat with a Buranese fisherman. The monastery has been renovated, and the Franciscan friars offer guided visits in Italian (www.sanfrancescodel deserto.it; Tue–Sun 9–11am, 3–5pm; donation appreciated; return taxi trip around €100 for 4).

Mosaic of the Last Judgement in Santa Maria dell'Assunta

Santa Maria dell'Assunta

Carry on down the same path to where the settlement began: the cathedral of **Santa Maria dell' Assunta** ❿ (Piazza di Torcello; tel; 041-730 119; daily Mar–Oct 10.30am–5.30pm, Nov–Feb until 5pm; charge, a combined ticket covers the cathedral, bell tower and museum). The oldest church in Venice, it was founded in ad639 but rebuilt between the 9th and 11th centuries. Note the foundations of the original baptistery on your left as you enter and the massive, 11th-century stone slabs acting as shutters on the south side of the cathedral.

The interior is impressive, and its lovely mosaics are among the oldest and finest in Italy. Most striking of all is *The Virgin and Child*, set against a glowing gold background in the dome of the central apse. The bell tower, offering stirring views of the lagoon, is currently closed for restoration but is scheduled to reopen in 2014.

Other highlights

The church of **Santa Fosca** ⓫ (daily 10am–4.30pm), which adjoins the cathedral, was built in the 11th century to enshrine the body of Santa Fosca, a Christian martyr. Close by, the weathered stone chair known as **Attila's Seat** is associated with the king of the Huns. According to local folklore, if single people sit on Attila's Seat they will be married within the year.

The nearby **Museo di Torcello** ⓬ (Tue–Sun Mar–Oct 10.30am–5.30, Nov–Feb 10am–5pm; charge) contains local archaeological finds and salvaged Byzantine mosaics. Dusk, when the sun is setting over the lagoon, is a beautiful time to return to Venice, unless you go back to Torcello (to Venissa) for dinner and catch a late ferry back.

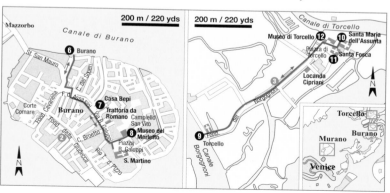

The Lido stretches over 11km (7 miles)

THE LIDO

Leave the sights of the city, catch a vaporetto to Venice's main bathing resort and cool off in the Adriatic. The long strip of land, around 11km (7 miles), protecting the Venetian lagoon from the Adriatic Sea, was Italy's first Lido. Enjoy its Belle Epoque architecture and maybe go for a cycle ride along the sea.

DISTANCE: 6km (4 miles)
TIME: A full day
START: Piazzale Santa Maria Elisabetta
END: Grand Hotel Excelsior
POINTS TO NOTE: Unless indulging in a motor launch, take a ferry (Nos 1, 2 or, in summer only, 5.1, 6) from Riva degli Schiavoni to the Lido. Nos 1, 2, 51, and 61 also go from Piazzale Roma. Young families usually love the Lido but avoid summer Sundays, when the Venetians flock here. The island has buses and taxis, but a bike is the best way of getting around. Try Lidoonbike (www.lidonbike.it) near the ferry stop, which hires bikes from around €10 a day (tandems and family bikes available).

In the 19th century, when the Lido was no more than a spit of sand, Byron, Shelley and other Romantics came here to escape the city. By the turn of the 20th century it was one of the most fashionable resorts in Europe, with the name applied to dozens of bathing resorts globally.

Given the urban nature of Venice, a summer dip at the Lido still provides a cooling-off experience, while the 15-minute ferry ride across the lagoon is a breeze. Helping to preserve this landscape is the new MOSE mobile dam, built across the Lido entrance to the lagoon.

All ferries arrive at **Piazzale Santa Maria Elisabetta ①**, where the sight of cars may come as a culture shock. From here, you can take a bus or taxi, hire a bike or walk to the eastern side of the island via the **Riviera Santa Maria Elisabetta**. The first landmark is the Tempio Votivo, commemorating the victims of both world wars. Many of the houses that line this seafront stretch were built in the 1920s, and reflect the fashion for reinterpreting Byzantine and Gothic Venetian architecture.

SAN NICOLÒ

Continuing along the lagoon shore, you will reach the church and Benedictine monastery of **San Nicolò ②** (Piazzale San Nicolò; 9am–noon, 4–7pm). From the church there are good views of the

The bronzed and beautiful

Fortezza di Sant' Andrea, a huge bastion on the island of Le Vignole built between 1535 and 1549 to guard the main entrance of the lagoon. Once a year, the doge would attend Mass at San Nicolò after the annual Marriage of the Sea ritual in the Porto di Lido. From the ceremonial stage barge he would cast a gold ring into the water, symbolising the marriage of Venice with the sea.

Nowadays Venice needs more than the doge's blessing to save it from serious floods so the city has turned to MOSE (Moses), the flood barrier being erected in the lagoon nearby.

JEWISH CEMETERIES

Head back along the Riviera San Nicolo, turning left on to Via Cipro for the **Antico Cimitero Ebraico ❸** (Old Jewish Cemetery; guided tours by appointment only, in English May–Oct, 2nd and 4th Sun of month, 3.30pm). The Jewish community was granted use of this land in 1386, which reflects the status of Jews in Venice at the time – segregated even in death, they were rowed down the Canale deglie Ebrei to the Lido, the cemetery for outcasts. Although the cemetery is seldom open to the public, there is free access to the Catholic and New Jewish Cemeteries nearby. Continue along Via Cipro for Via F. Duodo, where you can either stop for lunch at **La Favorita**, see ❶, or turn left and head for the beaches.

THE SEASIDE

For the full Italian beach scene, join the bronzed Euro-set at the Lido beach clubs from June to August. Daily hire of facilities are high, but, if you arrive after 2pm on weekdays, the beach fees are negligible and include parasol and beach bed. To avoid paying, stay by the water's edge of any hotel beach or head for the inevitably packed public beach

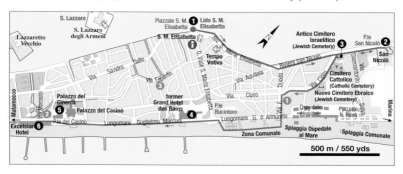

San Nicolò monastery   *Along Lungomare G. Marconi*

by the Blue Moon complex at the southern end of the Gran Viale Santa Maria Elisabetta. Best of all get on your bike for the more remote Alberoni beach at the southern tip of the Lido, with pine forests and rolling dunes.

Lungomare G. Marconi

The smarter stretch of beach abuts **Lungomare G. Marconi**, the boulevard with the grandest hotels and finest beaches. Taking centre stage is the Residenze de Bains, formerly the **Hôtel des Bains** ❹. This was the Lido's most glamorous landmark, immortalised by Thomas Mann in his 1912 novella *Death in Venice*. Italian director Luchino Visconti's 1971 screen adaptation, starring Dirk Bogarde as Aschenbach and filmed on the island, evokes the Lido's *dolce vita* days. Sadly the hotel went out of business in 2010 and has been converted into private apartments.

Lido Palazzi

Further along the seafront, the former **Palazzo del Casinò** (now a congress centre) and **Palazzo del Cinema** ❺ embody the Fascist architecture of the 1930s. In early September, celebrities flock to the latter for the Film Festival (see page 23).

End your seaside outing by admiring the exuberant, neo-Byzantine facade of the glamorous **Excelsior Hotel** ❻. The hotel's chic Blue Bar, popular with celebrities during the film festival, is, reportedly home to Venice's best Martinis. If staying on the island for dinner pop across to **La Tavernetta**, see ❷, or stop off at **Trattoria Andri**, en route back to the vaporetto stop, see ❸.

Food and Drink

❶ LA FAVORITA

Via Francesco Duodo; tel: 041-526 1626; closed Mon and lunch Tue and Jan–mid-Feb; €€€

The Lido isn't renowned for gastronomy, but this is one of its more upmarket restaurants, both for food and setting. In summer sit under pergola and tuck into lagoon seafood and fish dishes, accompanied by fine wines.

❷ LA TAVERNETTA

Via F. Morosini; tel: 041-526 1417; (opening times to come); closed winter; €€

This small welcoming restaurant offers Tuscan and Venetian cuisine. It's very popular during the Film Festival and has signed photos on the walls of film stars who have eaten here. Great wines.

❸ TRATTORIA ANDRI

Via Lepanto 21; tel: 041-526 5482; open Wed–Sun; €€

This pleasant canalside trattoria offers straightforward lagoon cuisine. Tuck into hearty platters of grilled or fried fish, as well as seafood salads and a refreshing house sorbet to finish.

The view from the Basilica San Marco

VENICE IN A DAY

Around 7 million people a year (about half the city's visitors) are day-trippers. If you are among this number and want to do a whistle-stop tour, follow this route, which pulls together highlights from many of the others in this guide.

DISTANCE: 3km (2 miles)
TIME: A full day
START/END: Stazione Ferroviaria Santa Lucia
POINTS TO NOTE: It is a good idea to buy a 24-hour vaporetto ticket (see page 36), since you will be using this mode of transport several times during the day. You can easily start at Piazzale Roma, where you can catch the No. 1 vaporetto. To condense the day due to time constraints, travel via vaporetto No. 2, which makes fewer stops. If you have more time, you can always add a more in-depth exploration of southern Dorsoduro (see page 57) or head back towards San Rocco and take in the church of the Frari and the San Polo district (see page 65).

GRAND CANAL AND RIALTO

Start at the **Stazione Ferroviaria Santa Lucia ❶** (Train Station), taking either the No. 1 vaporetto on the 13-minute ride to the Rialto Mercato stop. Take in the fantastic architecture found along the Grand Canal, looking out for ornate tracery on the Gothic palace of Ca' d'Oro (see page 38 and 77).

Rialto markets

Disembark at **Rialto Mercato ❷**, walk straight ahead into Campo Bella Vienna, and, if you arrive on any day other than Sunday, drink in the sights, smells, and sounds of the famous Rialto market (see page 70). The Rialto, the first area in Venice to be populated, has long been the commercial heart of the lagoon.

First, turn left and take the time to wander through the Erberia (page 70). Heading back into Campo Bella Vienna, turn right onto the Casaria, which will take you through the stalls and towards the two covered **Pescheria ❸** (Fish Market; Tue–Sat; see page 70). The market makes an inviting place to stock up on snacks for the next leg of your trip.

From the Pescheria, take any street on your left then head south down Ruga degli Speziali, the street of the spice

Sculpture of Adam on the Palazzo Ducale

traders, where you may catch a whiff of fresh coffee beans and the spices that are still sold from an ancient spice shop. If you want to have a coffee or glass of Garganega wine, perhaps with some traditional *cicchetti*, wander over to tiny **All'Arco**, see ❶.

Rialto Bridge

Returning to Ruga degli Speziali, continue south down Ruga dei Orefici, past the church of San Giacomo di Rialto (the oldest church in Venice, see page 72), and over the **Ponte di Rialto** ❹ (see page 72), the only permanent crossing point on the Grand Canal until the 19th century, making it an important location for merchants.

Fondaco dei Tedeschi

Straight ahead, the building standing slightly to the left is the **Fondaco dei Tedeschi** ❺ (see page 73), with its distinctive five large, rounded arcades. At one time the Germans used this edifice as their warehouse, mercantile offices and as lodging for Germans trading in the lagoon.

SAN MARCO

Coming straight off the bridge down Salizzada Pio X brings you to the San Marco district (see pages 28 and 46), most famous for its bustling Piazza, but also containing a cluster of other fine attractions.

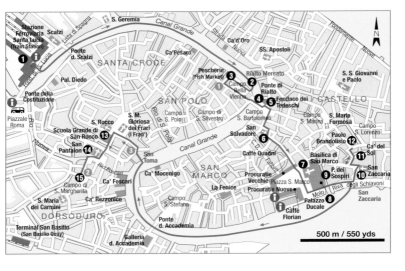

Ever-busy Piazza San Marco

San Salvadore

Turn right down the Marzarietta (also known as Via 2 Aprile), until you reach the church of **San Salvadore** ❻ (Campo San Salvadore; Mon–Sat 9am–noon, 3–6pm, Sun 3–7pm). The church, built in the 16th century, contains two lovely works by Titian, an *Annunciation*, in the third altar to the left, and *The Transfiguration*, at the high altar. The tomb of Caterina Cornaro, queen of Cyprus, can be found in the south transept.

Coming out of the church, take the Mercerie San Salvadore south as far as Piazza San Marco, reached through the archway of the clock tower, the Torre dell'Orologio (see page 34).

Piazza San Marco

You have now arrived in what is the only square worthy of the title piazza in Venice. For centuries this has been the gravitational centre of Venice. Napoleon called it 'the most elegant drawing room in Europe', although this does make one wonder why he then proceeded to hack down one end of it – now the site of the Ala Napoleonica (Napoleonic Wing) – destroying in the process Sansovino's church of San Geminiano.

If you have time, you could enjoy a spritz, a traditional aperitif, or a Prosecco, at one of the cafes on the square, such as **Caffè Quadri** (see page 108), or its rival, **Caffè Florian** (see page 35).

Basilica San Marco

Next stop is the **Basilica San Marco** ❼ (see page 28). To maximise your time, make sure to reserve tickets with Alata (www.alata.it). Alternatively, and if you have luggage, check it in at the nearby Ateneo Basso (just off Piazzetta Leoncina on Calle San Basso), and you will get a tag that allows you to skip the queue.

Once the private chapel of the Venetian doge, the basilica is decorated to impress. Visits last only about 10 minutes, as you are shuffled along a roped-off route, but you will still have time to take in the impressive mosaic interior of this sumptuous shrine. Make sure you pop into the Museo di San Marco, where you can view the four bronze horses originally brought back from Constantinople to crown the main door of the basilica (the ones currently outside are copies), as well as fantastic views over the square.

Saving San Marco

Beloved by Venetians, St Mark's bell tower (the Campanile, see page 30) is known as *'il paron de casa'* (the master of the house) but so far has not proved very masterful. When the tower was reconstructed in 1909, cracks appeared almost immediately as the new and old foundations were mismatched, despite the use of traditional materials and methods, such as placing foundations on a raft of larchwood. The *campanile* has been reinforced

The Bridge of Sighs   *The winged lion, emblem of Venice*

with titanium rods to prevent a second collapse.

Palazzo Ducale
You don't really have time on this tour to go into the **Palazzo Ducale** ❽ (see page 32), but you can, of course, still admire the glorious Gothic facade, where white stone and pink marble are used to dazzling effect. If you have time, take a closer look at some of the column capitals that ring the building. In the left-hand corner, closest to the Basilica San Marco, is a depiction of the *Judgement of Solomon*. Other capitals depict professions, animals and goods that were typical in the Republic of Venice, all showing the use of architecture to promote civic glory.

Exit the square in the direction of the lagoon, passing two columns topped by San Teodoro, the former patron saint of Venice, and the Winged Lion, the symbol of St Mark, the current patron saint of the city.

The Molo and Bridge of Sighs
Turn left onto the quayside, known as the Molo, the waterfront closest to the Basilica and look across the lagoon for views of the lovely island of San Giorgio Maggiore (see page 61). Standing on the crowded Ponte della Paglia, you will catch a glimpse of the restored **Ponte dei Sospiri** ❾ (Bridge of Sighs; see page 33), constructed to transport criminals from the prisons to the adjoining law courts.

CASTELLO

After crossing the Ponte del Vin, duck under the second *sottoportego* on your left and you will soon find yourself in Campo San Zaccaria. You are now in the Castello district (see page 50), the largest of the city's *sestieri*. Beyond the busy waterfront of Riva degli Schiavoni, the district is a good place to experience everyday Venetian life, with dark alleys opening into bright squares, pretty canals and some of the most impressive churches in the city.

San Zaccaria
Much of the land here was once owned by the convent of San Zaccaria, a nunnery that took in the most privileged women in Venetian society, often against their will. Drop into the church of **San Zaccaria** ❿ (see page 50), especially to view the moving *Sacra Conversazione* by Giovanni Bellini, in the second altar on the left.

Mask-makers
One cannot appreciate Venice without also appreciating the strong history of craftsmanship in the city. Leave the square by the archway in the northern corner, turn right into Campo San Provolo, under a *sottoportego*, and you will arrive at the Fondamenta dell'Osmarin. On the right you will see **Ca' del Sol** ⓫, at No. 4964 (www.cadelsolmascherevenezia.com). This mask workshop carries on the long-standing tradition of hand-craft-

Inside the Ca' del Sol mask workshop

ing papier-mâché masks, often based on characters from the *commedia dell'arte* (see page 21). The idea of anonymity created by the masks appealed to the Venetians, especially during carnival, since it allowed classes to mingle freely.

Gondola workshops

Just across the street, down the narrow Calle Corte Rota, you will find the workshop of **Paolo Brandolisio** ⑫ (No. 4725). Paolo is a *remèri*, the name for an artisan who creates *forcole* (the sculptural oarlock necessary for rowing gondolas) and oars. This is one of just four Venetian workshops that produce this part of the gondola. The *forcola* is crafted by hand from a single block of wood, either walnut, cherry or pear, and its finely sculptured shape allows for the correct movement of the oar.

Don't expect your questions answered unless you intend to buy a miniature oarlock as a souvenir, but you can certainly watch from the doorway. However, if you catch the artisans during downtime, they may be happy to answer questions.

At this point, retrace your steps to the Molo, then walk east, along the Riva degli Schiavoni. From here, catch the No. 1 or 2 vaporetto from **San Zaccaria** up the Grand Canal to the **San Tomà stop**, enjoying the scenery en route.

SAN POLO

The vaporetto deposits you in the San Polo district, which curves into the left bank of the Grand Canal. It is home to two of the city's greatest sights: the Frari, a huge Franciscan church containing masterpieces by Titian and Bellini, and the Scuola di San Rocco.

Scuola Grande di San Rocco

From the vaporetto landing, go straight ahead and turn right into Campo San Tomà. Follow the signs out of the square to reach Tintoretto's masterpiece, the **Scuola Grande di San Rocco** ⑬ (see page 65). The Florentine art historian Vasari referring to Tintoretto's works of art here wrote of 'the most extraordinary brain that the art of painting has produced' and three centuries on Ruskin, also a devotee, described San Rocco as having one of the three most precious picture collections in Italy.

DORSODURO

The remainder of this tour will mostly be spent exploring the western part of the artistic Dorsoduro neighbourhood, fuelled by the infusion of students at the Ca' Foscari University.

Take the Calle Fianco della Scuola beside the Scuola, then cross the bridge and at the end turn left and immediately right into Calle San Pantalon; this brings you into the square of the same name. **San Pantalon** ⑭ (Campo San Pantalon; Mon–Sat 8–10am, 4–6pm) has a huge awe-inspiring ceiling painted by Gian Antonio Fumiani.

The Grand Canal and La Salute church

It took him 24 years (1680-1704) to complete but then allegedly fell to his death from the scaffolding. On the left-hand side of the square, close to the canal, note the old slab that lists varieties of fish and the minimum sizes they had to reach before they were allowed to be sold.

Campo di Santa Margherita

Cross the bridge over the Rio Foscari and walk to the **Campo di Santa Margherita** 🕔, a large sprawling 'square' bustling with Venetian life. This is the hub of western Dorsoduro where locals come for the fish, fruit-and-vegetable stalls, university students for the bars, pizzerias and second-hand book stalls. A good spot to relax after an intense day of walking is **Caffè Rosso**, see ❷, on the square.

Once you've had a chance to rest your weary feet and enjoy a spot of people-watching – this area is usually very lively with locals – retrace your steps to the San Tomà vaporetto. Just before you get to the landing stage, at Campo San Tomà, you may be tempted by an early evening meal at the Trattoria San Tomà, see ❸, if you happen to have time in hand. To reach the railway station (or the nearby bus station) by boat from here, allow yourself approximately 30 minutes.

Food and Drink

❶ ALL'ARCO

San Polo 436, Calle dell'Occhialer; tel: 041-520 5666; Mon–Sat 8am–3pm (closed evenings); €
In the warren of the Rialto, this tiny *bacaro* sets out a few tables in summer, which are fought over by regular customers. The friendly father-and-son team serve some of the best (and best-value) *cicchetti* in town, as well as delicious *crostini*. Ingredients are all fresh from the Rialto markets.

❷ CAFFÈ ROSSO

Dorsoduro 2963, Campo Santa Margherita; tel: 041-528 7998; www.cafferosso.it; closed Sun; €

Head for the historic red café in the rambling Santa Marherita square and join students and *professori* from the nearby Ca' Foscari university. It's a great spot for a pre-dinner spritz, perhaps with a platter of crostini.

❸ TRATTORIA SAN TOMÀ

San Polo 2864/A, Campo San Tomà; tel: 041-523 8819; closed Tue; www.trattoriasan toma.com; €€
Tables here spill outside on to the pretty piazza and little garden. It's a friendly, welcoming spot where you can tuck into *misto di pesce* (seafood antipasti), taglioni with prawns and zucchini or simply grilled seabass. Unusally for Venice there's a good choice of salads. Pizzas are also an option.

DIRECTORY

Hand-picked hotels and restaurants to suit all budgets and tastes, organised by area, plus select nightlife listings, an alphabetical listing of practical information, a language guide and an overview of the best books and films to give you a flavour of the city.

Junior Suite at the Luna Baglioni

ACCOMMODATION

Venice excels at cultural one-upmanship. You can sleep in Tchaikovsky's bed or wake up in palaces that welcomed doges, Henry James and Hemingway. If you hanker after decadence and drama, choose a grand pile on the Grand Canal. If you yearn for a quiet life, chiming bells and secret gardens, slip into a family-owned *palazzo* in the backwaters of Cannaregio. Or, for a sense of Venice before the interior decorators moved in, retreat to a bucolic inn in Burano, the lagoon's friendliest island.

Venice is over-burdened with palatial piles, but there is now great choice at the more modest end, from boutique retreats to chic guesthouses, eclectic B&Bs, Gothic apartments, or intimate, family-owned *palazzi*.

The lack of standardisation cuts both ways: each room is delightfully different but, on the other hand, even in a distinguished hotel, the rooms at the front may be glorious, but hide dingy garrets at the back.

Apartments: A delightful way of experiencing the city, even revelling in a Gothic *palazzo* complete with gondola dock. **Venetian Apartments** (www.venice-rentals.com) are the market leaders.

B&Bs: This is an effective way of getting to meet local people. For a wide range of B&Bs, see BB Planet (www.bbplanet.com) and check by district and price; also see the Venice tourist board website (www.turismovenezia.it).

Outside Central Venice: Apart from Giudecca, consider the islands of Burano, Murano and the Lido. If you are staying outside the city, avoid soulless Mestre and opt for Padua or Treviso, a 30-minute train ride from Venice.

Tourist tax: Be prepared for the tourist tax introduced in 2011, which applies to hotels and B&Bs (hostels are exempt). The cost, payable by cash only, depends on the hotel and season but is typically €3 per person per night for a 3-star hotel, €4 for a 4-star. It is payable on the first five nights only. Children below 10 are free, 10- to 16-year-olds pay half.

Price for a double room with breakfast for one night in high season, excluding city tax.
€€€€ = over 400 euros
€€€ = 300–400 euros
€€ = 160–300 euros
€ = below 160 euros

San Marco

La Fenice et des Artistes
Campiello della Fenice; tel: 041-5223 2333; www.fenicehotels.com; vaporetto San Marco or Santa Maria del Giglio; €€
Within a stone's throw of La Fenice

Opera House, this hotel is popular with singers and musicians. There is a new and an old section, both furnished in traditional style.

Flora

Calle dei Bergamaschi, off Calle Larga XXII Marzo; tel: 041- 520 5844; www.hotelflora.it; vaporetto: Santa Maria del Giglio; €€

This is a charming, sought-after, family-run hotel in a quiet spot near St Mark's. Bedrooms can be palatial or poky (try No. 32 that leads to the garden). Breakfast is taken in the secluded courtyard garden.

Gritti Palace

Campo Santa Maria del Giglio; tel: 041-794 611; www.thegrittipalace.com; vaporetto: Santa Maria del Giglio; €€€€

Hemingway, Churchill and Greta Garbo all stayed in this 15th-century palace. The most patrician hotel in Venice, it retains the air of a private *palazzo*, with Murano chandeliers and damask furnishings. It reopened after a year-long restoration in spring 2013.

Hotel Albergo San Samuele

Salizzada San Samuele; tel: 041-520 5165; www.hotelsansamuele.com; vaporetto: San Samuele. €

Tucked away behind Palazzo Grassi, this central, budget hotel has charming service, provided by a hands-on owner, sunny, pared-down rooms and free WiFi. It's great value for this arty area

Locanda Art Deco

Calle delle Botteghe; tel: 041-277 0558; www.locandaartdeco.com; vaporetto: Sant'Angelo or Accademia; €€

This is a quiet, good-value B&B within a 17th-century palace just off Campo Santo Stefano. All rooms come with personal computer and free WiFi.

Locanda Novecento

Calle del Dose; tel: 041-241 3765; www.locandanovecento.biz; vaporetto: Santa Maria del Giglio; €€€

This ethnic-chic boutique hotel offers an exotic touch of Marrakech, with funky Moroccan lamps and Turkish rugs. There are beamed ceilings, cosy bedrooms and a tiny courtyard for breakfast.

Locanda Orseolo

Corte Zorzi; tel: 041-520 4827; www.locandaorseolo.com; vaporetto: San Marco. €€

This friendly, family-run hotel lies behind Piazza San Marco and is made up of three family-run guest houses. Staff are exceptionally helpful. Cosy, traditional, Venetian-style rooms overlook canal or courtyard.

Luna Baglioni

Calle Larga dell' Ascensione; tel: 041-528 9840; www.baglionihotels.com; vaporetto: San Marco; €€€€

The oldest hotel in Venice, this was originally a Knights Templar lodge for pilgrims en route to Jerusalem. Just off Piazza San Marco, it has Venetian decor, an

18th-century ballroom and the grandest breakfast room in Venice.

Monaco e Grand

Calle Vallaresso; tel: 041-520 0211; www.hotelmonaco.it; vaporetto: San Marco; €€€€

A mix of slick contemporary and classic Venetian style, with a chic bar and waterfront breakfast room. The Palazzo Salvadego annexe is more typically Venetian, and less expensive (€€€), but shares the same smart breakfast room.

Santo Stefano

Campo Santo Stefano; tel: 041-520 0166; www.hotelsantostefanovenezia.com; vaporetto: San Samuele or Accademia; €€

Set in a 15th-century watchtower overlooking one of the city's most stylish squares, this restructured hotel has a friendly, unjaded attitude. Bathrooms come with marble mosaics, jacuzzi and Turkish bath.

Saturnia & International

Calle Larga XXII Marzo; tel: 041-520 8377; www.hotelsaturnia.it; vaporetto: Santa Maria del Giglio; €€€

The mood of this distinctive hotel is vaguely medieval in inspiration which, depending on your mood, can be romantic or austere. Bedrooms are intimate and comfortable.

Westin Europa & Regina

Corte Barozzi, off Calle Larga XXII Marzo; tel: 041-240 0001; www.starwoodhotels.com; vaporetto: San Marco; €€€€

With a lovely waterfront position facing La Salute Church this 18th-century palace has been renovated, and the stuccowork and damask tapestries shown off to greater effect. Bedrooms are spacious, and decorated in Venetian style.

Castello

Bed and Breakfast San Marco

Fondamenta San Giorgio degli Schiavoni; tel: 041-522 7589; www.realvenice.it; vaporetto: San Zaccaria. €

Set on the third floor, this basic but friendly B&B offers rooftop or canal vistas, but it's also about the location: five minutes from St Mark's. Breakfast is taken in a communal kitchen. Its sister B&B is featured on the same website.

Casa Querini

Campo San Giovanni Novo; tel: 041-241 1294; www.locandaquerini.com; vaporetto: San Zaccaria or Rialto; €€

This small inn close to Campo Santa Maria Formosa has 11 spacious, low-key rooms, decorated in 17th-century Venetian style. Pleasant staff.

Colombina

Calle del Rimedio; tel: 041-277 0525; www.colombinahotel.com; vaporetto: San Zaccaria; €€

This boutique hotel close to St Mark's offers balconies with views of the Bridge of Sighs and a muted, modern take on Venetian style.

Terrace with unbeatable views at the Luna Baglioni

Danieli

Riva degli Schiavoni; tel: 041-522 6480;
www.starwoodhotels.com/danieli;
vaporetto: San Zaccaria; €€€€

Set on the waterfront, this world-famous hotel has a splendid Gothic foyer, and plush rooms with parquet floors and gilded bedsteads. Doge Dandolo used to live here; Dickens, Wagner, Ruskin and Balzac are among the many famous names on the guest list. Choose the *Casa Vecchia* doge's residence not the 'Danielino' 1940s extension. The views are spectacular from the rooftop bar and restaurant, La Terrazza. Unless you are a celebrity guest, or huge tipper, the hotel service can be supercilious.

Gabrielli

Riva degli Schiavoni; tel: 041-523 1580;
www.hotelgabrielli.it; vaporetto: San
Zaccaria; €€

This family-run waterfront hotel in a Gothic palace is seemingly mired in a delightful 18th-century time warp. Breakfast and candlelit dinners are taken in a flowery courtyard, and views can be enjoyed from the panoramic roof terrace.

Liassidi Palace

Ponte dei Greci; tel: 041-520 5658;
www.liassidipalacehotel.com; vaporetto:
San Zaccaria; €€€

This boutique hotel in a Gothic palace behind the Riva degli Schiavoni has a muted yet sleek interior. The individual-istic bedrooms range from Art Deco to Bauhaus.

Locanda La Corte

Calle Bressana; tel: 041-241 1300;
www.locandalacorte.it; vaporetto:
Ospedale; €€

Off Campo SS Giovanni e Paolo this is a small Gothic palace with bedrooms overlooking the canal or courtyard, where breakfast is served The decor is a muted version of the traditional Venetian style.

Locanda Vivaldi

Riva degli Schiavoni; tel: 041-277 0477;
www.locandavivaldi.it; vaporetto: San
Zaccaria; €€€

Facing the lagoon, the hotel is partially set in the house where Vivaldi once lived. Bedrooms are romantic and individualistic, and many have jacuzzis. Breakfast is take on the roof terrace. No guesses as to the background music.

Londra Palace

Riva degli Schiavoni; tel: 041-520 0533;
www.londrapalace.com; vaporetto: San
Zaccaria; €€€€

Londra Palace, where Tchaikovsky composed his *Fourth Symphony*, is a grande dame, with 100 windows overlooking the lagoon. A room with a view will transform your stay. For drama and waterside bustle, get a fourth-floor room overlooking the lagoon. Or hide out under the eaves on the fifth

Palazzo keys

floor, where 502 has views across the lagoon to San Giorgio.

Metropole

Riva degli Schiavoni; tel: 041-520 5044; www.hotelmetropole.com; vaporetto: San Zaccaria; €€€€

This boutique hotel is dotted with eclectic antiques and objets d'art. It has a Michelin-starred restaurant, a trendy bar, lovely garden courtyard and lagoon or canal views; rooms can be cosy (No. 350) or amusingly kitsch (No. 251).

Palazzo Schiavoni

Fondamenta dei Furlani; tel: 041-241 1275; www.palazzo schiavoni.com; vaporetto: San Zaccaria; €€

Rooms and apartments in a tasteful conversion (with the odd frescoed ceiling) beside the Scuola di San Giorgio. A good choice for families.

La Residenza

Campo Bandiera e Moro; tel: 041-528 5315; www.venicelaresidenza.com; vaporetto: San Zaccaria or Arsenale; €€

This pared back yet atmospheric 15th-century palace is set on a pleasant square off the tourist trail, yet only a stone's throw from the Riva degli Schiavoni. Even if the 15 bedrooms are a touch spartan, the public rooms are decorated with antiques, chandeliers and old paintings. It is a quiet, inconspicuous hotel, which appeals to independent travellers.

Residenza de l'Osmarin

Calle Rota; tel: 347 450 1440; www.residenzadelosmarin.com; vaporetto: San Zaccaria: €

Enjoying proximity to Piazza San Marco, but on a charming neighbourhood quayside, this recently opened B&B has spotless, good-value guest rooms (one with its own panoramic terrace) and friendly, helpful owners.

Ruzzini Palace

Campo Santa Maria Formosa; tel: 041-241 0447; www.ruzzini palace.com; vaporetto: Rialto: €€€

This 17th-century *palazzo* overlooking a charming square was abandoned for decades, then in 2008, after nine years of restoration, was given a second lease of life as a luxury hotel. The breakfast has a chic, contemporary design, but elsewhere the style is classic Venetian with some fine frescoes, original beamed ceilings and paintings of Venice in her heyday.

Santa Marina

Campo Santa Marina; tel: 041-523 9202: www.hotelsantamarina.it; vaporetto: Rialto; €€€

Located between the bustling Rialto and Campo Santi Giovanne e Paolo, this is a pleasant if slightly lacklustre hotel, redeemed by friendly, helpful staff. Breakfast is taken on the terrace. The rooms in the annexe are slightly cheaper (€€).

Balcony blooms

Dorsoduro

Accademia Villa Marevege

Fondamenta Bollani; tel: 041-521 0188; www.pensioneaccademia.it; vaporetto: Accademia; €€€

This gracious, highly sought-after wisteria-clad villa was once the Russian Embassy. It is located at the Grand Canal end of Rio San Trovaso, with delightful gardens where breakfast is served in summer, and sunsets are toasted in style. Atmospheric bedrooms vary in size and style.

Bloom/7 Cielo

Campiello Santo Stefano 3470, tel: 340 149 8872; www.settimocielo-venice.com; vaporetto: Accademia; €€

Overlooking Campo Santo Stefano, these twin B&Bs are set on the upper floors of a grand *palazzo* but are different in mood. **7 Cielo** (Seventh Heaven) is overtly romantic, with Murano-tiled bathrooms and moody bedrooms. **Bloom** is distinctly Baroque, with bold colours and gilded beds.

Ca' della Corte

Corte Surian; tel: 041-715 877; www.cadellacorte.com; vaporetto: Ferrovia; €

A quiet and friendly B&B in a 16th-century *palazzo* with private terrace. It offers a variety of accommodation and, despite its secluded setting, is very handy for the station and Piazzale Rome.

Ca' Maria Adele

Rio Terrà Catecumeni; tel: 041-520 3078; www.camariaadele.it; vaporetto: Salute; €€€€

This boutique gem beside La Salute offers Baroque glamour, bohemian charm and canalside views. The Doge's Room is a riot of red brocade; the Sala dei Mori has lovely views. Attentive staff.

Ca' Pisani

Rio Terrà Foscarini; tel: 041-240 1411; www.capisanihotel.it; vaporetto: Accademia or Zattere; €€€

In a historic *palazzo* near the Accademia, this is a glamorous, Art Deco-style retreat, rather retro despite WiFi throughout. Other touches include peaceful patio breakfasts, and the hip wine bar/restaurant.

Ca' San Trovaso

Fondamenta delle Eremite; tel: 041-241 2215; www.casantrovaso.com; vaporetto: Ca' Rezzonico or San Basilio; €

This unpretentious little hotel on a quiet canal has terracotta floors and damask wallpaper, but no TV or phones in rooms. Nice roof terrace.

Charming House DD.724

Ramo de Mula 724; tel: 041-277 0262; www.thecharminghouse.com; vaporetto: Accademia; €€€

This sleek, modernist-chic designer retreat is quirky and cosy enough to appeal to old Venetian hands. Consider

A typical Venetian room

DD.694, the sister apartment nearby, and a similar retreat in Castello.

Don Orione

Rio Tera Foscarini; tel: 041-522 4077; www.donorione-venezia.it; vaporetto: Accademia; €

On a square near the Accademia, this former orphanage and monastery is now a superior hostel run by a religious foundation. The tranquil gardens and Gothic cloisters are open to guests. Expect comfortable rooms, private bathrooms and a restaurant.

Locanda San Barnaba

Calle del Traghetto; tel: 041-241 1233; www.locanda-sanbarnaba.com; vaporetto: Ca' Rezzonico; €€

This small inn near Ca' Rezzonico occupies a 16th-century frescoed palace run by the ancestral owner. Rooms are Venetian-style, a few with balconies, and there is a pretty canalside courtyard for breakfast.

Pensione La Calcina

Fondamenta Zattere ai Gesuati; tel: 041-520 6466; www.lacalcina.com; vaporetto: Zattere; €€

With wonderful views looking across the canal to Giudecca, this romantic inn is where the art historian John Ruskin lodged in 1876. La Piscina restaurant, with tables on a pontoon, is a lovely spot for lunch or candlelit dinner. Book early, especially for a room with a view. Apartments nearby are also available

Pensione Seguso

Fondamenta Zattere ai Gesuati; tel: 041-528 6858; www.pensionesegusovenice.com; vaporetto: Zattere; €

This old-fashioned *pensione*, with wonderful views, dates back to the early 20th century when a British diplomat converted the 16th-century building into a hotel. It attracts many of the same guests year after year.

Cannaregio, San Polo and Santa Croce

3749 Ponte Chiodo

Ponte Chiodo; tel: 041-241 3935; www.pontechiodo.it; vaporetto: Ca' d'Oro; €

Located in the quiet Cannaregio backwaters, this is a budget guesthouse offering rare amenities such as WiFi and air conditioning. The friendly owner may eat breakfast with his guests and provide valuable information about the city.

Abbazia

Calle Priuli dei Cavaletti; tel: 041-717 333; www.abbaziahotel.com; vaporetto: Ferrovia; €€

Set close to the Ca' d'Oro, this romantic 16th-century palace features stuccoed salons adorned with School of Tintoretto paintings and Murano chandeliers, matched by frescoed, silk-lined bedrooms and sumptuous beds. Canal views and a secret garden complete the picture.

Palazzi line the canals

Ca' d'Oro

Corte Barbaro; tel: 041-241 1212;
www.venicehotelcadoro.com; vaporetto:
Ca' d'Oro; €€
Set in an historic palazzo near the Ca'
d'Oro ferry stop, this quiet, cosy hotel
offers a range of rooms from tiny to
grand.

Ca' Gottardi

Strada Nuova; tel: 041-275 9333;
www.cagottardi.com; vaporetto: Ca' d'Oro;
€€
Overlooking the busy Strada Nuova, this
is an elegant and friendly little hotel but
don't expect spacious rooms.

Ca' Pozzo

Sottoportego Ca' Pozzo, Ghetto Vecchio;
tel: 041-524 0504; www.capozzoinn.com;
€€
This small, simple hotel is modern and
minimalist in style with pastel hues,
exposed beams and modern art.

Ca' Sagredo

Campo Santa Sofia; tel: 041-241 3111;
www.casagredohotel.com; vaporetto: Ca'
d'Oro; €€€€
Ca' Sagredo occupies an historic Grand
Canal *palazzo* adorned with fabulous
frescoes by Tiepolo and Sebastiano
Ricci. Many rooms have Grand Canal
views; you can breakfast under a Tiepolo ceiling, sip cocktails at the canalside bar. The hotel can also provide a
babysitter, personal shopper or personal trainer on request.

Casa del Melograno

Campiello del Ponte Storto; tel: 041-520
8807; www.locandadelmelograno.it;
vaporetto: San Marcuola; €
Tucked away off the busy Strada Nuova
shopping street, this is a great budget
option, with a garden, and rooms remodelled in a simple modern style.

Domus Orsoni

Corte Vedei; tel: 041-275 9538;
www.domusorsoni.it; vaporetto: San
Marcuola; €€
Set near the Ghetto, this stylish, mosaic-
studded guesthouse belongs to a mosa-
ic-producing company with the only
furnace allowed to function in central
Venice; attractive walled garden; try a
mosaic course too.

Giorgione

Santi Apostoli; tel: 041-522 5810;
www.hotelgiorgione.com; vaporetto: Ca'
d'Oro; €€
Not far from the Ca' d'Oro, this family-
run, 15th-century *palazzo* is excellent
value for a 4-star hotel. Decor is traditional Venetian, with chandeliers and
Murano glass; the breakfast room opens
onto a courtyard.

Grand Hotel Dei Dogi

Fondamenta Madonna dell'Orto; tel: 041-
220 8111; www.boscolohotels.com; €€€€;
vaporetto: Madonna dell'Orto
This is a grand hotel marooned on the
edge of the lagoon. A former monastery,
it is still an oasis of calm, with tasteful

Venetian decor and the largest, loveliest hotel garden in Venice; courtesy motor-boat shuttle.

Locanda Antico Doge

Campo Santi Apostoli; tel: 041-241 1570; www.anticodoge.com; vaporetto: Ca' d'Oro; €€

On a busy but pleasant square this palazzo once housed Doge Marino Falier. Expect damask-draped bedrooms, gilt mirrors and original antiques.

Locanda Leon Bianco

Corte Leon Bianco; tel: 041-523 3572; www.leonbianco.it; vaporetto: Ca d'Oro: €€

This is a simple, friendly hotel overlooking the Grand Canal and entered through a tucked-away courtyard. Three of the seven rooms have canal vistas and are excellent value. Breakfast is served in rooms.

Locanda ai Santi Apostoli

Strada Nuova; tel: 041-0996 916; www.locandasantiapostoli.com; vaporetto: Ca' d'Oro; €

This discreet family-run inn is on the third floor of a 14th-century palazzo overlooking the Grand Canal (room 11 has the best view).

Palazzo Abadessa

Calle Priuli, tel: 041-241 3784; www.abadessa.com; vaporetto Ca' d'Oro; €€€

Tucked away behind Ca' d'Oro, this romantic boutique hotel is both patrician and homely, with breakfast amid birdsong in the walled garden, and guests plied with Prosecco. The house-party mood survives stuccoed salons adorned with School of Tintoretto art and Murano chandeliers, matched by frescoed, silk-lined bedrooms and sumptuous tester beds. Best bedrooms are the frescoed, green-damasked junior suites (23 and 21).

San Cassiano (Ca' Favretto)

Calle della Rosa; tel: 041-524 1788; www.sancassiano.it; vaporetto: San Stae or Ca' d'Oro via gondola ferry; €€

This Grand Canal hotel, with a gondola jetty, has much faded charm. Half the rooms have canalside views across to the Ca' d'Oro but vary dramatically in size and price.

The Giudecca

Bauer Palladio Hotel & Spa

Fondamenta della Croce, Isola della Giudecca; tel: 041-520 7022; www.bauervenezia.com; vaporetto: Zitelle; €€€

Set in Palladio-designed cloisters, this serene, somewhat austere space has garden terraces, canalside views and a special spa; courtesy shuttle boat to the more worldly Bauers Hotel over the water. Closed mid-winter.

Casa Genoveffa

Calle del Forno, Giudecca 472; tel: 347 250 7809; www.casagenoveffa.com; vaporetto: Palanca. €

Lavish room at the Cipriani

Tucked away down a back alley, this unpretentious but cosy B&B has beamed rooms and four-poster beds.

Cipriani

Isola della Giudecca 10; tel: 041-240 801; www.hotelcipriani.com; vaporetto: Zitelle; €€€€

Beloved by movie stars, the Cipriani can be seen as a cliché, but it conveys a sense of warmth and intimacy better than most other grand hotels. Expect a busier mood in the main hotel compared with the self-contained Palazzo Vendramin. Complimentary motor launch to St Mark's.

Hilton Molino Stucky

Isola della Giudecca 753; tel: 041-272 3311; www.molinostuckyhilton.com; vaporetto: Palanca; €€€

This formidable-looking flour mill on the Giudecca waterfront is a luxury hotel with a rooftop pool, magical terrace and the cool Skybar lounge. A spa, several restaurants and a ground-floor bar add to the holiday feel. Complimentary shuttle boat to St Mark's.

Murano, Burano and Torcello

Locanda Cipriani

Piazza Santa Fosca, Isola di Torcello; tel: 041-730 0150; www.locandacipriani.com; vaporetto: Torcello €€

This bucolic inn beloved by Hemingway is set in a remote spot. Run by a branch of the Cipriani family, it boasts a celebrated homely restaurant, with a garden for outdoor dining (closed Jan and Tue).

Murano Palace

Fondamenta Vetrai 77, Isola di Murano; tel: 041-739 655; www.murano palace.com; vaporetto: Colonna; €€

Overlooking the splendid Rio dei Vetrai (Glassmakers' Canal) on Murano, this is a rewarding, under-priced gem, with splendid Murano chandeliers and a refined 18th-century Venetian decor. Enjoy sailing, rowing and fishing, and the family's restaurant nearby.

Venissa

Fondamenta Santa Caterina, Isola di Mazzorbo (Burano); tel: 041-527 2281; www.venissa.it; vaporetto: Mazzorbo; €€

Run by the Bisol Prosecco dynasty, this peaceful, rural guesthouse, gourmet restaurant and wine estate revels in creative cuisine (see page 82).

The Lido

Rivamare

Lungomare Marconi 44, Lido; tel: 041-5260352; www.hotelrivamare.com; vaporetto: Lido; €

This welcoming, family-run beach hotel is perfect for young families. Some rooms have sea views and small balconies and there's a summer terrace. There is a separately run meditation centre.

Pricey cafés line Piazza San Marco

RESTAURANTS

Venetian restaurants range in style from cool, 18th-century elegance – especially in San Marco and Castello – to rustic gentility. Yet individualistic inns abound, tucked under pergolas or spilling onto terraces and courtyards. More up-market places are termed *ristoranti*, but may be called *osterie* (inns) if they focus on homely food in an intimate or rustic setting. *Bacari* are traditional wine bars that also serve food, a Venetian version of tapas, known as *cicchetti*.

Always book in advance for fancier restaurants, and, because local people flock to high-quality, but reasonably priced, eateries, especially at weekends, reservations are advisable in general.

Most restaurants close between lunch and dinner sittings. Lunch is normally served between 12.30pm and 2.30pm, with dinner service starting around 7pm. Late-night dining can be difficult to find, so you will generally need to settle on somewhere by 9pm. Where no times are given in these listings, restaurants are open daily for lunch and dinner.

San Marco

A Beccafico
Campo Santo Stefano, San Marco 2801; tel: 041-527 4879; www.abeccafico.com; vaporetto: Accademia; €€
For a change from Venetian fare, try the Sicilian specialities such as the mussel soup under the pastry top or the vermicelli with sardines and wild fennel. A relative newcomer to Campo Santo Stefano, the restaurant has tables on the square and is the perfect spot for watching the world go by on a warm day.

Acqua Pazza
Campo Sant'Angelo, San Marco 3808; tel: 041-277 0688; all day 10am–11pm; vaporetto: S. Angelo; €€
This slick, upmarket spot on a trendy square is the place for huge pizzas or fine seafood when Venetian squid ink is too exotic to contemplate. A post-coffee Limoncello is on the house.

Alla Basilica
Calle Albanesi, Castello 4255; tel: 041-522 0524; Tue–Sun, noon–3pm; www.allabasilicavenezia.it; vaporetto: San Zaccaria; €
A stone's throw from Piazza San Marco this canteen-like trattoria offers fantas-

Price guide for a two-course meal for one with a glass of house wine:
€€€€ = over €85
€€€ = €55–85
€€ = €30–55
€ = up to €30

Venetian sweet

Piazza San Marco waiter

tic value for central Venice. The fixed price (lunch only) menu at €14 includes a pasta and main course, cover and service. It's good, unfussy fare.

Antico Martini

Campo Teatro Fenice; San Marco 2007; tel: 041-522 4121; www.anticomartini.com; vaporetto: S.M del Giglio; €€€€

This classic restaurant, with piano bar and late opening hours, is a Venetian institution. The menu includes seafood risotto, *granseola* (spider crab), châteaubriand and *fegato alla veneziana* (liver on a bed of onions). Good food and service and an extensive wine list ensure a regular clientele.

Le Bistrot de Venise

Calle dei Fabri, San Marco 4685; tel: 041 523 6651; www.bistrotvenise.com; vaporetto: San Marco; €€€

Set behind St Mark's, this romantic wine-bar and bistro is a touch touristy, but redeemed by the canalside terrace, fine wines and seafood staples such as lobster and scampi.

Caffè Centrale

Piscina Frezzeria, San Marco 1659b; tel: 041-887 6642; daily 6.30pm–1am; vaporetto: San Marco; €€€

This sleek lounge bar and late-night restaurant feels more Milanese or Manhattanite than Venetian, albeit with gondola attached. The moody palazzo mixes modish cuisine and cutting-edge design.

Cavatappi

Campo della Guerra, near San Zulian, San Marco 525; tel: 041-296 0252; closed Sun D and Mon; vaporetto: San Zaccaria or Rialto; €

A fashionable, contemporary-style wine bar serving *cicchetti*, light lunches and evening meals. Good specials.

Club del Doge

Hotel Gritti Palace, Campo Santa Maria del Giglio, San Marco 2467; tel: 041-794 611; vaporetto: S. M. del Giglio; €€€€

Enjoy traditional food in a palatial setting overlooking the Grand Canal, with probably the best terrace in town. It's equally atmospheric for lunch or drinks.

De Pisis

Hotel Bauer, Campo San Moise, San Marco 1459; tel: 041-520 7022; daily; vaporetto San Marco; €€€€

Expect dazzling damask and candlelight, with views from the terrace of the Grand Canal and service and food to match. A dash of Asian influence is added to the Mediterranean flavours.

Enoteca Al Volto

Calle Cavalli 4081; tel: 041-522 8945; daily 10am-4pm, 6–10pm; vaporetto: Rialto; €

This is the place for wine by the glass accompanied by *cicchetti* or a more substantial bowl of pasta. The outdoor tables are soon snapped up, but the back room is cosy, with a nautical feel. Cash only.

Spider crab at Da Fiore

Grancaffè Quadri and Ristorante Quadri

Procuratie Vecchie, Piazza San Marco; tel: 041-522 2105; summer daily, Tue–Sun in winter; €€ café, €€€€ restaurant

On the floor above the famous Grancaffè Quadri, founded in 1638 there is now an elegant gourmet restaurant run by a 3-star Michelin chef – with views over San Marco to match. Booking is essential.

Grand Restaurant

Hotel Monaco and Grand Canal, Calle Vallaresso, San Marco 1332; tel 041-520 0211; vaporetto: San Marco; €€€€

This elegant terrace restaurant (with piano bar) has fine views over the lagoon, taking in La Salute and San Giorgio. International, Italian and Venetian dishes include fish soup, vegetable risotto and scampi. Booking required.

Harry's Bar

Calle Vallaresso, San Marco 1323; tel 041-528 5777; daily 10.30am–11pm; www.harrybarvenice.com; vaporetto: San Marco; €€€€

This legendary bar and restaurant is consistently good and draws a Venetian crowd. The unpretentious tone is perfect, set by the current Arrigo (Harry) Cipriani. Sip a Bellini (Prosecco and peach juice, invented here). Booking is essential.

Osteria Ai Assassini

Rio Terrà degli Assassini; San Marco 3695; tel: 041-528 7986; closed Sun; vaporetto: S. Angelo; €€

This lively *bacaro* has been here over 100 years. Menus change daily and depend on the day of the week: meat specialities Monday to Wednesday, fish Thursday to Saturday. Both come highly recommended.

PG's Restaurant

Palazzina Grassi, San Marco 3247; tel: 041-528 4644; closed Mon; www.palazzinag.com; vaporetto: San Samuele. €€€€

Set in a Philippe Starck-designed boutique hotel halfway down the Grand Canal, this seductive gastro temple appeals to the art and film crowd. Reserve.

Sangal

San Marco 1089; tel: 041-319 2747; closed Tue; www.sangalvenice restaurant.com; vaporetto: San Marco; €€€€

A stone's throw from Piazza San Marco, this designer restaurant/lounge bar draws the fashionable crowd for the sophisticated cuisine, central location and top-floor terrace. Prices here, whether for full meals or cocktails, are not for the faint-hearted.

Castello

Al Covo

Campiello della Pescaria, Castello 3968; tel 041-522 3812; closed Wed and Thur; www.ristorantealcovo.com; vaporetto: Arsenale; €€€

Al fresco drinks

Covo's fine reputation draws foodies to sample the fish-heavy tasting menu. The *moeche* (softshell crab) lightly fried with onions vie with Adriatic tuna, or squid-ink pasta with clams and courgette flowers. Booking is essential.

Al Mascaròn

Castello 5225, Calle Longa Santa Maria Formosa; tel: 041-522 5995; Mon–Sat; €€
Although no longer a secret, and no longer cheap, this homely yet arty *osteria* is still friendly and dependable, with hearty, straightforward dishes ranging from Adriatic fish to the freshest *antipasti*, bean soup and mixed grills. Save room for the delicious Burano biscuits dipped in dessert wine.

Alle Testiere

Calle del Mondo Novo, Castello 5801; tel: 041-522 7220; closed Sun and Mon; www.osteriaalletestiere.it; vaporetto: Rialto or San Zaccaria; €€€
Near Campo Santa Maria Formosa, this consistently good seafood restaurant requires booking. It has very few tables and, unusually for Venice, two sittings in the evening. The menu recalls Venice's days on the oriental spice route; little razor clams (capelonghe) or pasta may be subtly spiced. Great wine list.

La Corte Sconta

Calle del Pestrin, Castello 1621; tel: 041-522 7024; closed Sun and Mon; vaporetto:

Arsenale; €€€
An authentic seafood spot, tucked in a secret courtyard, with a cheerful atmosphere and a menu based on fish fresh from Chioggia market. Tuck into infinite courses of fishy *antipasti*, from scallops and mantis shrimps to sardines and baby crabs. Book.

Do Leoni

Hotel Londra Palace, Riva degli Schiavoni, Castello 4171; tel: 041-520 0533; www.londrapalace.com; vaporetto: S. Zaccaria; €€€€
The waterfront restaurant maintains its Venetian character while satisfying international tastes. Fans of Venetian food with a contemporary twist can sample sarde in saor and risi e bisi as well as seafood grills and gnocchi with shrimps. There's an informal mood on the terrace. Live music in the evenings.

Enoteca Mascareta

Calle Lunga Santa Maria Formosa, Castello 5183; tel: 041-523 0744; open evenings only, 7pm–2am; vaporetto: Rialto; €€
A cosy, rustic wine bar run by convivial wine writer Mauro Lorenzon. Nibble on *charcuterie* at the counter, or choose from the small menu.

Hosteria da Franz

Salizada San Antonin, Castello 3499; tel: 041-522 0861; closed Tue; www.hostariadafranz.com; vaporetto:

Venetian cod speciality

Giardini; €€€

Sample Venetian seafood dishes with a twist, from risotto to gnocchi with prawns and spinach, marinated prawns or simply grilled fish. It's off the beaten track, but handy for the Biennale. Booking is advisable.

Osteria Al Mascaron

Calle Longa Santa Maria Formosa, Castello 5225; tel: 041-522 5995; closed Sun; www.osteriamascaron.it; vaporetto: Rialto; €€

Set in a lively area, this is an ideal introduction to a Venetian inn. An old-fashioned, gentrified-rustic wine bar and inn, it offers friendly but leisurely service, fine wines and reliable cooking. Try the antipasti, the bean soup, and the mixed grill; and save room for the delicious Burano biscuits dipped in dessert wine.

Osteria di Santa Marina

Campo Santa Marina, Castello 5911 tel: 041-528 5239; closed Sun, and Mon lunch; vaporetto: Rialto; €€€

Set in a quiet square, this deceptively simple trattoria presents reinterpretations of Venetian classics, from cuttlefish-ink ravioli with sea bass to fresh turbot, beef carpaccio or tuna and bean soup. In summer, sit outside and finish with a cinnamon apple pie.

Ristorante Giorgione

Via Garibaldi, Castello 1533/38; tel: 041-522 8727; closed Wed; www.ristorantegiorgione.it; vaporetto: Giardini; €€

Set in the working-class Arsenale area of Eastern Castello, this inn is popular with Venetians, both for the traditional fish recipes and the live folk music. Lucio Bisutto, the owner for 20 years, plays his guitar and sings Venetian songs most nights.

Dorsoduro

Ai Gondolieri

Dorsoduro 366, Ponte del Formager; tel: 041-528 6396; www.aigondolieri.it; Wed–Mon; €€€

Old-school formality and, unusually for Venice, a fish-free, meat-based menu, which is strong on lagoon vegetables and pasta.

Avogaria

Calle del'Avogaria, Dorsoduro 1629; tel: 041-296 0491; closed Mon; vaporetto: San Basilio; €€

With exposed brickwork, cool clientele and creative *cicchetti*, Avogaria is more than a modish tapas bar. After a few slivers of fishy delights, you might find yourself settling in for the risotto.

La Bitta

Calle Lunga San Barnaba, Dorsoduro 2753a; tel: 041-523 0531; closed for lunch and all day Sun; vaporetto: Ca' Rezzonico; €€

An unpretentious, good-value little restaurant, which, unusually for Venice, concentrates on meat dishes; in fact

Chic and elegant Dorsoduro

Grilled shrimp make for a great starter

no fish at all. Steak, chicken, goose and fegato alla veneziana (calves' liver with onions) are among the well-cooked offerings.

Cantinone già Schiavi

Fondamenta Nani, Dorsoduro 992; tel: 041-523 0034; closes 9.30pm and Sun dinner; vaporetto: Zattere; €

This old-fashioned canalside wine bar is popular with Venetians and visitors alike. It's a good place for *cicchetti* – among the most inventive in Venice. Prop up the bar over a light lunch or linger over canalside cocktails (7–8pm).

Da Montin

Fondamenta delle Eremite, Dorsoduro 1147; tel: 041-522 7151; closed Tue dinner and Wed; www.locandamontin.com; vaporetto: Zattere; €€€

This enchanting but over-priced arty garden restaurant was once favoured by such luminaries as Hemingway and Peggy Guggenheim. Although it is most popular in summer, the cosy, faintly bohemian dining room comes into its own in winter.

La Furatola

Calle Lunga San Barnaba, Dorsoduro 2869; tel: 041-520 8594; closed Thur and lunch Mon; vaporetto: Ca' Rezzonico; €€€

A cosy place renowned for fish, all fresh from the Rialto. Wonderful desserts too.

Linea d'Ombra

Dorsoduro 19, Ponte dell'Umiltà, Zattere; tel: 041-2411 881; Wed–Mon; €€€

Facing the Il Redentore church on the Giudecca, this romantic restaurant and wine bar is perfect on a summer's evening, especially if you can secure a table on the pontoon. Creative cuisine and vaguely reinterpreted Venetian classics, including seabass in a crust or tuna tartare. Book in summer.

Oniga

Campo San Barnaba; tel: 041-522 4410; closed Tue; www.oniga.it; vaporetto: Ca' Rezzonico; €€

Eat inside or on the campo, opting for the seafood platter or the vegetarian option. Vegetarians can be spoilt with pasta dishes made with artichokes, aubergines and pecorino cheese. Excellent wine list, with 150 labels.

Quattro Feri

Calle Lunga San Barnaba, Dorsoduro 2754; tel: 041-520 6978; closed Sun; vaporetto: Ca' Rezzonico; €€

This bustling new-wave bacaro attracts a faithful young crowd to sample Venetian dishes and superior wines.

The Giudecca

Altanella

Calle delle Erbe; tel: 041-522 7780; closed Mon and Tue; vaporetto: Palanca or Redentore; €€€

This friendly trattoria, with outdoor seating over a picturesque canal, has been

run by the same family for over 100 years. Fish dishes and seafood pastas predominate. The ice cream with grappa-soaked raisins makes a delightful dessert. Cash only.

Do Mori

Fondamenta Sant'Eufemia; tel: 041-522 5452; closed Sun; vaporetto: Palanca; €€

Formed by a breakaway group from Harry's Bar, this is the place for those who can't afford the elevated prices of the original. The food is sound Venetian home cooking, with a preponderance of fish dishes (good scampi risotto) plus pasta and pizzas.

Fortuny Restaurant

Hotel Cipriani, Fondamenta San Giovanni; tel: 041-520 7744; closed Nov–Mar; vaporetto: Zitelle; €€€€

The Fortuny spills onto a glorious terrace: the setting is exquisite, the formal service divine and the prices deadly. Or try the more informal (and relatively less pricey) **Cip's Club** (€€€). Both offer views across to San Marco and free launch service from St Mark's pier. Book ahead.

Harry's Dolci

Fondamenta San Biagio; tel: 041-522 4844; closed Mon and Tue and Nov–Mar; www.cipriani.com; vaporetto: Palanca; €€€

Come here for a waterside American brunch; it's Harry's without the hype, and with better views and prices. Try the Venetian risotto, come for cakes (*dolci*)

outside meal times, or sip a signature Bellini in the bar.

La Palanca

Fondamenta al Ponte Piccolo; tel: 041-528 7719; Mon–Sat L only; vaporetto: Palanca; €

This friendly neighbourhood bar-trattoria, always full of locals, serves a short lunch-time menu. Grab one of the outdoor tables and enjoy sweeping views across to Venice over a plate of risotto in cuttlefish ink or tagliatelle with porcini mushrooms.

San Polo, Santa Croce and the Rialto

Al Nono Risorto

Sottoportego della Siora Bettina, Campo San Cassiano; tel: 041-524 1169; closed all day Wed and Thur lunch; vaporetto: San Silvestro; €€

This is a rustic spot, framed by a wisteria-hung courtyard and garden. With its radical-chic mood, it is particularly popular with thirty-something Venetians. Try the squid with polenta or one of the excellent pizzas.

Al Prosecco

Santa Croce 1503, Campo San Giacomo dell'Orio; tel: 041-524 0 222; www.alprosecco.com; Mon–Sat; €€

Friendly brother owners Stefano and Davide run this small *enoteca*. A great selection of wines by the glass (including superior Prosecco) accompany gen-

A staple accompaniment to any Venetian meal

erous platters of cheeses, *salumi* (cold cuts), smoked fish, crostini and salads, all sampled in a charming neighbourhood campo.

Al Vecio Fritolin

Calle della Regina, Santa Croce 2262; tel: 041-522 2881; closed Mon, and Tue lunch; www.veciofritolin.it; vaporetto: San Stae; €€€

Irina's cosy, quirky fish restaurant near the Rialto Bridge is the place for a seafood extravaganza, but it can also be the scene of a more modest pasta lunch. The full menu features mixed fried fish, soft-shell crab and swordfish tartare.

All'Arco

Calle dell'Occhialer, San Polo 436 ; tel: 041-520 5666; open Mon–Sat 8am–3pm; vaporetto: Rialto Mercato; €

This tiny, hard-to-find bacaro is packed with both locals and tourists, who come at lunch for the renowned *cicchetti* and cheap glasses of Prosecco. The father-son team produce a whole range of Venetian snacks from *baccalà mantecato* (creamy salt cod) and *sarde in soar* (marinated sardines) to delicious cured meats and crostini.

Alla Madonna

Calle della Madonna, San Polo 594; tel: 041-522 3824; closed Wed; www.ristoranteallamadonna.com; vaporetto: Rialto Mercato; €€

This bustling, ever-popular trattoria serves meticulously prepared seafood. Tuck into Sant'Erasmo artichokes or a seafood risotto and be seduced by the impressive art collection (no bookings).

Alla Zucca

Ponte del Megio, off Campo San Giacomo dell'Orio, Santa Croce 1762 tel: 041-524 1570; closed Sun and Aug; vaporetto: San Stae; €€

This popular trattoria is set by a crooked canal bridge, with a few tables outside. The bohemian atmosphere reflects the vegetable-inspired menu (aubergine pasta, smoked ricotta, pumpkin flan) as well as meat and fish. Book at least 24 hours in advance.

Antica Bessetta

Salizzada de Ca' Zusto; tel: 041-721 687; closed Tue and lunch Wed; www.anticabessetta.com; vaporetto: Riva di Biasio; €€€€

Off the beaten track, just north of San Giacomo dell'Orio, this is a rustic-style trattoria, but standards, and prices, are high. It is a temple of Venetian home cooking and a foodies' paradise, with *risi e bisi* (rice and peas), gnocchi, seafood risotto; or the catch of the day, grilled or baked, accompanied by distinctive regional wines.

Antiche Carampane

San Polo 1911; Rio Terà delle Carampane; tel: 041-524 0165; www.antichecarampane.com; Tue–Sat;

Al fresco dining

€€€

Not easy to find, but worth the search because the seafood dishes are excellent, even if service for tourists doesn't always come with a smile. You can eat at outside tables in summer.

Cantina Do Spade

Calle delle Do Spade, Rialto, San Polo 860; tel: 041-521 0583; www.cantinadospade.com; vaporetto: Rialto Mercato; €

This is one of the oldest Rialto *bacari*, still going strong and run by a friendly young team keen to tempt you with deep-fried *calamari, baccalà* (salt cod), meatballs and other typical Venetian *cicchetti*. Stand at the bar or grab a table for a traditional meal.

Da Fiore

Calle del Scaleter, off Campo di San Polo; tel: 041-721 308; closed Sun, and Mon lunch; www.dafiore.net; vaporetto: S. Tomà; €€€€

Regularly dubbed the best restaurant in town, this is a celebrity haunt during the Film Festival. At best, Da Fiore reflects the subtlety of Venetian cuisine, from *grilled calamari* and *granseola* (spider crab) to Adriatic tuna, sashimi and *risotto al nero di seppia* (cuttlefish risotto). Only one (much sought-after) table overlooks the canal.

Da Pinto

Campo delle Beccarie, San Polo 367; tel: 041-522 4599; open for meals daily 10am–10pm; www.vinidapinto.it; vaporetto: Rialto Mercato; €

This historic Rialto market inn has been restored, revealing a huge fireplace in the medieval meathouse. Snooty local people say the *osteria* has sold out by offering pizza, but they still serve cichetti at the bar or a generous menu (pasta and fish for €20–25). You can eat seated beneath exposed beams or outside on the market square.

Frary's

Fondamenta dei Frari, San Polo 2559; tel: 041-720 050; closed Tue; vaporetto: S. Tomà; €

Facing the Frari church, this cosy, reliable Arab and Greek restaurant aspires to a 'thousand-and-one-nights' atmosphere. Dishes run from Greek salad and moussaka to an array of Lebanese mezze (a selection of small dishes) and fish couscous.

Il Refolo

Campiello del Piovan, Campo San Giacomo dell'Orio; tel: 041-524 0016; closed all day Mon and Tues lunch; closed winter; €–€€

In a pretty canalside setting, this innovative, upmarket pizzeria is the place for a peaceful candlelit dinner in an out-of-the-way spot. Outdoor seating only.

Ristorante Ribot

Fondamenta Minotto, Rio del Gaffaro, Santa Croce 160; tel: 041-524 2486; closed

Sun; www.ristoranteribot.com; vaporetto: Piazzale Roma or San Tomà; €€

This authentic neighbourhood restaurant is superb value (try the risotto, grilled scallops or seafood pasta). It also has a secret garden, and in the evening, a warm atmosphere, thanks to the live music and friendly service.

Taverna del Campiello Remer

Cannaregio 5701; Campiello del Remer; tel: 041-522 5789; www.alremer.com (for useful map); closed Wed and Sun lunch; €€

This hard-to-find *taverna* is deservedly popular for its romantic canalside setting, mellow mood and generous food. A stylish crowd come for the good-value lunch-time buffet ; Happy Hour with *cicchetti* (5.30–7.30pm); and live music every night, from piano to soul or jazz. Only book for the *à la carte* restaurant.

Cannaregio

Ai Promessi Sposi

Calle dell'Oca, Cannaregio 4367; tel: 041-241 2747; closed Mon, and Wed lunch; vaporetto: Ca' d'Oro; €

This busy little osteria serves a wide selection of *cicchetti*, plus clams, pasta and *pasticcio di crespelle al pesce* (fish pancakes) and *castraure* (baby artichokes).

Algiubagio

Fondamente Nuove 5039; tel: 041-523 6084; closed Tue; www.algiubagio.net;

vaporetto: Fondamente Nuove; €€ (lunch) €€€ (dinner)

This contemporary quite elegant restaurant with a waterfront terrace in summer is a good spot for lunch while waiting for the ferry to the islands. It is popular with the locals and the wide-ranging menu offers seafood, home-made pasta, steaks and vegetarian dishes.

Alla Frasca

Campiello della Carità, Cannaregio; tel: 041-528 5433; closed Mon and Wed lunch; vaporetto: Fondamente Nuove; €€

Hidden in the backstreets, this friendly, neighbourhood inn serves fresh, no-frills food at decent prices; eat grilled fish or spaghetti with clams in the pretty courtyard and feel like a Venetian.

Al Vecio Bragozzo

Strada Nuova , Cannaregio 4386; tel: 041-523 7277; closed Mon; vaporetto: Ca' d'Oro; €€

It can be hard to distinguish among the tourist places that lie along the Strada Nuova, but this restaurant caters to both locals and tourists and has a huge selection of seafood.

Alla Vedova

Cannaregio 3912, Ramo Ca' d'Oro; tel: 041-528 5324; closed Thur and lunch Sun; €€

This atmospheric, time-worn inn is known for its wines and hearty *cic-*

Colourful Burano

chetti, including delicious hot *polpette* (meat balls). Full seafood meals and pasta dishes are also on offer. Book in advance.

Anice Stellato

Fondamenta della Sensa, Cannaregio 3272; tel: 041-720 744; closed Mon–Tue; www.osterianicestellato.com; vaporetto: Guglie or Sant'Alvise; €€

This small, family-run restaurant is a long way from the centre but always busy (book if you can). Come for the *cicchetti* or for a full meal, including pasta with prawns and courgette flowers. Spices are used widely, making for a quirky twist on Venetian cuisine, such as in sardines with ginger.

Bentigodi

Calleselle; Cannaregio 1423; tel: 041-822 3714; closed Sun; www.3bentigodi.com; vaporetto: Guglie; €

At the entrance of the ghetto, this is a cheery bacaro-cum-trattoria, serving a good selection of cheap cichetti plus main meals with Venetian specialities and dishes from southern Italy – the new chef is from Calabria.

Da Rioba

Fondamenta della Misericordia, Cannaregio 2553; tel: 041-524 4379; closed Mon; www.darobia.com; vaporetto: San Marcuola; €€

This rustic-chic osteria is set on a canal that comes alive at night, and you can dine outside, by the bustling water-front. The cooking is subtly creative, with pasta dishes or seafood, including tuna carpaccio.

Fiaschetteria Toscana

Salizzada San Giovanni Cristostomo, Cannaregio 5719; tel: 041-528 5281; closed all Tue, and Wed lunch; www.fiaschetteriatoscana.it; vaporetto: Rialto; €€€

Set near the Rialto Bridge, this is a local favourite for excellent seafood, plus a smattering of Tuscan steak dishes and cheeses, and fine wines. Book in advance.

Vini da Gigio

Fondamenta di San Felice, Cannaregio 3628; tel: 041-528 5140; closed Mon and Tue; www.vinidagigio.com; vaporetto: Ca' d'Oro; €€

Cosy and romantic, this popular family-run inn serves reliable Slow Food with leisurely service. Lots of variety, from Venetian risotto to northern Italian game dishes. Book in advance.

The Islands

Ai Frati

Fondamenta Venier, Murano; tel: 041-736 694; closed for dinner and all day Thur; www.aifrati.com; vaporetto: Murano; €€

The location and neighbourhood atmosphere make this fish restaurant very popular, so be sure to book. If you have the choice, try to get one of the tables on a mooring platform on the canal.

Burano is now known for its Slow Food inns

Ai Pescatori

Piazza Galuppi, 371, Burano; tel: 041-730 650; closed Tue; vaporetto: Burano; €€

This welcoming restaurant serves fish and game. Try the seafood risotto or tagliolini with cuttlefish.

Alla Maddalena

Fondamenta di Santa Caterina 7C, Mazzorbo; tel: 041-730 151; 8am–8pm; closed Thur; €€

At Burano, cross over the footbridge to Mazzorbo and enjoy a lazy lunch in this authentic trattoria. The superbly creative menu, based on seafood and game, is inspired by Veneto cuisine, Slow Food values and very local wines.

Da Romano

Via Galuppi 221, Burano; tel: 041-730 030; www.daromano.it; Wed–Mon, closed Sun dinner; €€

This welcoming fish restaurant, which has been here for over a century, is both hearty and arty. The interior is packed with paintings donated by visiting artists. The signature dish is the Gò risotto, made with stock from the eponymous fish found in the Venetian lagoon.

Locanda Cipriani

Piazza Santa Fosca 29, Torcello; tel: 041-730 150; www.locandacipriani.com; Feb–Dec Wed–Mon lunch; €€€

This rural retreat, run by the nephew of Arrigo Cipriani, the owner of Harry's Bar, is a local institution. Try the grilled fish, fillet steak or *risotto alla torcellana*. Book in advance.

Venissa

Fondamenta di Santa Catarina 3, Mazzorbo; tel: 041-5272 281; (Ferry 12 from Fondamenta Nuove, or cross the footbridge from Burano); Tue–Sun; closed mid-winter; www.venissa.it; €€€€

In a bucolic setting with its own vineyard and vegetable garden, this Michelin-starred restaurant on the little island of Mazzorbo feels a far cry from central Venice. Award-winning chef Antonia Klugmann has earned a Michelin star for exquisite fish and seafood dishes. Go with well-lined pockets, especially if you opt for the tasting menus (€75 and €95).

The Lido

Pachuka Beach

Via Ing.Klinger 1; tel: 041-770 147; open summer only, daily until late; vaporetto: San Nicolò; €

By day this is an enjoyable beach pizzeria/restaurant. The mood changes at sunset when the party starts, with disco or live music, dancing and occasional themed events.

La Taverna

Hotel Westin Excelsior, Lungomare Marconi 41; tel: 041-526 0201; vaporetto: Lido; €€€

This summery restaurant spreads out under a terrace overlooking the beach. There is a very good buffet with a range of delicious grilled fish. Booking essential.

All dressed up for a night out

NIGHTLIFE

Nightlife in Venice tends to be low-key, playing on romance, intimacy and charm rather than cutting-edge clubs and urban thrills. For smart nightlife call into the cocktails bars of the top hotels, or the historic cafés around San Marco. At the less formal end of the scale don't leave without popping into one of the city's *bacari*, or wine bars. Whether 'new-wave' or traditional, the bars will be bursting with tasty treats to detain you from dinner. The Rialto area is the best spot to embark on a *giro d'ombra* (wine crawl). In summer the nightlife scene switches to the Venice Lido and focuses on the seafront and the grand hotels. You may also find yourself rubbing shoulders with the glitzy set, especially during the film festival.

San Marco

B-Bar Lounge
Bauer Hotel, San Marco 1459; tel: 041-520 7022; www.bauerhotels.com; S.M. del Giglio
Celebrity types feel utterly at home in the B-Bar, where the gold mosaics reflect the glitterati in all their glory. Live music takes place most evenings, and there are DJs at weekends.

Hard Rock Cafe
Bacino Orseolo, San Marco; tel: 041-522 9665; www.hardrock.com; 11am–11.30pm (bar open later at weekends); vaporetto: San Marco
This new branch of the American music

café is the smallest one in Europe. Expect signature cocktails and classic burgers, with views over moored gondolas.

Harry's Bar
Calle Vallaresso, 1323; tel: 041-528 5777; all day, until 11pm; vaporetto: San Marco
Come here for atmosphere, the legendary Bellini cocktails and some celebrity spotting in surprisingly low-key, but often crowded surroundings. Food is also available, at eye-watering prices.

PalazzinaG
Ramo Grassi, 3247; tel: 041-528 4644; www.palazzinag.com; vaporetto: San Tomà
The hotel is home to several modish bars where a Philippe Starck makeover has created a clubby look with quirky Murano chandeliers and animal artworks in Carnival masks.

Castello

Enoteca Mascareta
Calle Lunga Santa Maria Formosa, 5183; tel: 041-523 0744; daily 7pm–2am; vaporetto: Rialto
The eccentric host, laid-back jazz and superb wines ensure a contented Venetian clientele at this busy wine bar.

San Polo

Al Bancogiro
Campo San Giacometto, 122; tel: 041-523 2061; www.osteriabancogiro.it; closed Mon;

Check out the lively bar scene   *San Marco's Caffè Florian goes all musical at night*

vaporetto: Rialto Mercato
One of the new-wave *bacari* that look traditional but have dared to redesign the menu to keep with the times. It's a lively canal-side spot for a spritz and, unusually for Venice, the restaurant opens until late.

Do Mori

Calle dei Do Mori, 429; tel: 041-522 5401; closed Sun; vaporetto: Rialto Mercato
This small picturesque *bacaro* is tucked away in the back alleys and crammed with locals for its excellent selection of wines by the glass, lively atmosphere and good *cicchetti* (snacks). Arrive by 6.30pm – it closes early and the food flies off the counter.

Dorsoduro

Cantinone Gia Schiavi

Fondamenta Nani, 992; tel: 041-523 0034; Mon–Sat till 9.30pm; closed Sun pm; vaporetto: Zattere
This simple neighbourhood bar is very popular for early evening canalside cocktails and creative *cicchetti*.

Margaret du Champ

Campo di Santa Margherita, 3019; tel: 041-528 6255; daily 10am–2am; vaporetto: Ca' Rezzonico
This cool venue is one of several late-night bars on this lively square.

Orange

Campo Santa Margherita, 3054; tel: 041-523 4740; closed Sun; vaporetto: Ca' Rezzonico

This contemporary lounge bar, with an in-house DJ, is one of the current hot-spots on the Campo.

Cannaregio

Casino di Venezia

Palazzo Vendramin-Calergi, Grand Canal; tel: 041-529 7111; www.casinovenezia.it; games rooms: Sun–Thur 3.30pm–2.30am, Fri and Sat 3pm–3am; slot machines open from 11am; vaporetto: San Marcuola
Entry to the casino allows you to appreciate the splendour of one of the finest palaces on the Grand Canal. The emphasis is on table games, though there are also American-style slot machines. Visitors need ID, and jackets are compulsory for men (provided free of charge).

Il Paradiso Perduto

Fondamenta Misericordia, 2540; tel: 041-7205 81; 7pm–1am (Sat till 2am), closed Wed; vaporetto: San Marcuola
This bohemian live music haunt on a sleepy canal wakes up at night. There is always background or live music (jazz, folk or ethnic) accompanied by hearty Venetian fare.

Giudecca

Skyline Rooftop Bar

Molino Stucky Hilton Hotel, Fondamenta San Biagio 810, Giudecca; tel: 041-272 3311; 5pm–1am and at lunchtime in summer; vaporetto: Palanca.
This stylish bar on the eighth floor of the Hilton Molino Stucky has a dazzling vista across the Giudecca Canal to Venice.

Colourful houses in Murano

A–Z

A

Age restrictions

While there is no law limiting the age for drinking alcohol in Italy, there is a law against serving alcohol to minors under 18 in restaurants, bars, etc. The legal driving age is 18. One can marry with court consent at 16 and without at 18.

B

Budgeting for your trip

To help with planning the trip, here is a list of approximate prices in euros.

Airport Transfer from Marco Polo. *By road*: public bus (ACTV) €6; taxi €50 (for up to four people). *By water*: Alilaguna public water launch from €30 return per person; private water taxi €110–200 one way for four people and luggage.

Entertainment. A concert in a main church costs from €25; Fenice opera tickets from €80. Casino admission €5.

Gondolas. From €80–150 (depending on duration, time of day and services).

Guided Tours. For walking tour allow around €25.

Food. *Tramezzini* (small sandwiches, at café and bar counters) from €2; *cicchetti* (tapas in wine bars) €1.50–4 each; full meal excluding drinks at inexpensive restaurant €30; moderate restaurant €5; pizza 810–15; beer €3–5; glass of house wine €2–5.

Hotel. For bed and breakfast per night in high season, including tax: deluxe €400 and above; expensive, €280–400; moderate, €140–280; inexpensive, less than €140. You can find some real bargains off-season (Nov, early Dec and mid-Jan to the Feb Carnival) with prices slashed by 50 percent or more.

Lido beaches (paying ones). From around €12 (including sunbed/parasol) but heavily reduced prices after 2pm.

Museums and Attractions. €4–20 but best to buy a museum pass – one for all civic museums costs €24, for museums of Piazza San Marco €18.

Public Transport. Vaporetto: €35 for 3 days, €25 for 36 hours, €20 for 1 day (24 hours).

C

Climate

Venetian winters are cold, summers are hot, and the weather the rest of the year somewhere in between. The winds off the Adriatic and occasional flooding mean Venice can be damp and chilly, although very atmospheric, between November and March. June, July and August can be stifling – air conditioning is pretty essential for a good night's rest at this time of year.

Gondolier in classic striped top and straw boater

Clothing

A pair of comfortable walking shoes is essential – despite Venice's excellent canal transport network, if you want to sightsee, you'll probably spend most of your time on foot. For summer, pack thin cotton clothing and a light jacket for breezy evening vaporetto rides. When visiting churches, your back and shoulders should be covered. In winter, pack layers, including a warm coat. Smart hotels lend boots and umbrellas in case of light flooding, but bring your own just in case.

Venice is generally an informal city, but stylish dress is expected at smarter restaurants and piano bars, including at the more elegant hotels. Men must wear a jacket for the Casino but these can be hired free of charge.

Crime and safety

Although Venice is incredibly safe, pickpockets are not uncommon, especially in crowded areas around the Rialto and San Marco. Carry only what is absolutely necessary; leave passports, airline tickets and all but one credit card in the hotel safe. If nervous, consider a money belt, and be careful on crowded public transport, especially getting on and off the vaporetti, around the train station and in San Marco.

Make photocopies of your passport and other vital documents to facilitate reporting any theft and obtaining replacements. Notify the police as soon as possible of any theft, so that they can give you a statement to file with your insurance claim.

Cruise Venice

The **Blue Alilaguna** route (www.alilaguna.it) links the Cruise Terminal to both San Marco and Marco Polo Airport. New cruise terminals reflect the huge popularity of cruising. Even if you only have one day in Venice, reliable transport links will help you get the most from a fleeting visit. The main Venice Cruise Terminal (**Terminal Venezia Passeggeri**) is close to the 4km (2-mile) causeway that links the historic city with the mainland. Centred on the **Bacino Stazione Marittima (Marittima Basin)**, it handles the largest ships. The additional **San Basilio Terminal** is closer to the main sights, just around the corner in the Giudecca Canal. The **Sette Martiri quays** near the Biennale gardens are mostly used by river cruises and smaller craft. For cruise information, including maps, see: www.vtp.it.

Customs and entry requirements

EU citizens: a valid passport or identity card is all that is needed to enter Italy for stays of up to 90 days. Citizens of Australia, Canada, New Zealand and the US require only a valid passport.

Visas. For stays of more than 90 days a visa (*permesso di soggiorno*) or residence permit is required. Regulations change from time to time, so check

The brand new People Mover

with the Italian Embassy (www.esteri. it) or in your home country before you travel.

Customs. Free exchange of non-duty-free goods for personal use is allowed between countries within the EU. Refer to your home country's regulating organisation for a current list of import restrictions.

Currency restrictions. Tourists may bring €10,000 cash (or equivalent in other currency) into the country.

D

Disabled travellers

With narrow alleys and stepped bridges, Venice is a challenge, especially if you are not travelling through a specialist tour operator or able to splash out on water taxis. Ideally, book through a specialist foreign operator, or even one on the ground. **Accessible Italy** (tel: +39 378 94 111, www. accessibleitaly.com) provides a comprehensive list.

But there are ways of getting around and seeing some of the major sights. For transport tips, see **Venice Connected** (www.veniceconnected.com) and check the 'Accessible Venice' section. As for hotels, avoid the Santa Croce and San Polo areas, which are unsuitable, and ideally opt for a Grand Canal hotel near a ferry stop or a hotel with a free water shuttle. For walks, ramps along the Zattere make this delightful stroll more accessible. **Citta per Tutti** has a use-

ful website at www.comune.venezia.it/ informahandicap and a branch at Ca' Farsetti, Riva del Carbon, San Marco 4136; tel: 041-274 8144/041-965 5440.

The main (but inevitably very busy) **tourist office** in the Venice Pavilion (see page 129) supplies maps with itineraries marking accessible areas, bridges with ramps for wheelchairs, and toilets for the disabled. Keys to operate the bridges are available from the tourist office, but it can be a saga. Accessible attractions (no differentiation is made between full and partial access) include the Basilica San Marco, Palazzo Ducale, Ca' Rezzonico, as well as the Frari and La Salute churches.

Driving

Venice is a traffic-free zone, and the closest you can get to the centre is Piazzale Roma, where there are two large multistorey car parks and good ferry services. There is also a huge multi-storey car park on the adjacent island of Tronchetto, the terminal for the car ferry to the Lido, where driving is allowed. Tronchetto (www. veniceparking.it) has been linked since 2010 to Piazzale Roma via the monorail, called the People Mover (www. asmvenezia.it). There are also good transport links to the Cruise Terminal. Although the outdoor car parks are guarded, it's sensible not to leave anything of value in your car.

Gondolas moored in winter

E

Electricity

The electrical current is 220V, AC, and sockets take two-pin round-pronged plugs. Bring an adaptor *(un adattatore)*, as required.

Embassies and consulates

Most have lists of English-speaking doctors, lawyers, interpreters, etc.

Australia (Consulate): Via Borgogna 2, Milan tel: 02-7767 4200, www.italy. embassy.gov.au.

Canada (Consulate): Riviera Ruzzante 25, Padua; tel: 049-876 4833.

New Zealand (Embassy): Via Clitunno 44, Rome; tel: 06-853 7501, www.nz embassy.com.

Republic of Ireland (Embassy): Villa Spada, Via Giacomo-Medici, Rome; tel: 06-585 2381, www.embassyof ireland.it.

South Africa (Consulate): Santa Croce 466/G, Piazzale Roma, Venice; tel: 041-524 1599.

UK (Consulate): Piazzale Donatori di Sangue 2, Mestre; tel: 041-505 5990, www.ukinitaly.fco.gov.uk.

US (Consulate): Via Principe Amedeo 2/10, Milan; tel: 02-290 351, http:// milan.usconsulate.gov.

Emergencies

Ambulance: 118; **Fire:** 115; **Carabinieri:** 112 (urgent police action); **Police:** 113

Experiences

Cookery courses: Chef and foodie expert Countess Enrica Rocca runs full-day cooking classes, including visits to the Rialto market. Courses in very small groups are held on Tuesdays and Saturdays and cost from €250 per person; half day classes on Wednesdays from €180 and Monday wine pairings from €230 (tel: + 39 338 634 3839; www.enricarocca.com for further information).

Cycling: While cycling is (sensibly) banned from Central Venice, the Lido makes a perfect cycling destination, if only for a day (or half-day) trip. Bikes can be picked up close to the Lido ferry stop.

Gondola tour with a twist: For an atmospheric, personalised gondola tour with the only female gondolier in Venice, known as *'La Prima Gondoliera'*, contact Alex Hai. You even get a bottle of Prosecco in the gondola (tel: +39 348 302 9067; email: primagondoliera@gmail. com).

Rowing, Venetian-style: Row Venice teaches Venetian rowing in a matter of hours: standing and facing forward and rowing using a long oar which rests on the special wooden oarlock known as the *forcola* (lessons from €40; contact Jane Caporal, Row Venice, tel: +39 347 7520 637, www.rowvenice.com, mailto:info@rowvenice.com)

Kayaking in Venice or the lagoon: Venice Kayak offers refreshingly untouristy

Palazzo Ducale façade detail

kayak tours around the city and lagoon, including seeing the sights from the water. Day trips for 2–5 cost €120 per person, half-day €90. (Contact Venice Kayak, tel: +39 346 477 1327, www. venicekayak.com.)

Venetian Club: a community-minded 'club' that tempts you to try out ancient Venetian crafts like ceramics or book-binding: www.thevenetianclub.co.uk.

F

Festivals and events

These are the main traditional festivities but Venetians love an excuse for a party or a water pageant so expect myriad smaller events.

February
Carnevale (Carnival). These pre-Lenten festivities are celebrated in unrivalled style in Venice (see page 20).

May
Festa della Sensa, Ascension Day. Venice celebrates its 'marriage with the sea' in a ceremony during which the mayor throws a ring into the water between St Mark's and the Lido. There's also a regatta pageant and rowing races.

Vogalonga. On 12 June. Hundreds of boats descend upon the waterways for a colourful 30km (18-mile) race (www. vogalonga.it).

June
Venice Biennale is a major contemporary art fair held from June–November in odd-numbered years and staged in the Biennale pavilions in the Giardini Pubblici (Public Gardens), the old Arsenale and other city locations (www.la biennale.org). In even numbered years the Architecture Biennale is held in the Giardini pavilions.

July
Festa del Redentore, on the third Saturday of July, celebrates the city's deliverance from the plague in 1567 with fireworks and a lagoon procession.

August/September
Venice International Film Festival. Usually the last few days of August and first week of September (www.la biennale.org).

Regata Storica. First Sunday in September. The Historical Regatta starts with the water pageant on the Grand Canal, followed by races in traditional boats.

November
La Festa della Madonna della Salute. Commemorating the city's deliverance from the plague of 1630.

G

Guides and tours

The tourist office (see page 129) can supply a list of qualified tour guides if you want a personal tour of a particular site or on a specialist aspect of Venice. All year round there are standard tours (book through hotels and travel agencies), including a two-hour walking tour of San Marco, taking in the Basilica and the Palazzo Ducale; a two-hour

The Regata Storica   *Ornate Carnival mask*

walking a tour covering the Frari and the Grand Canal; a three-hour islands tour; and even a ghost walk.

Accademia Gallery: for booking tickets at set times or for booking individual art tours (tel: 041-520 0345).

Brenta Canal cruise: a cruise to Padua aboard the 200-seater *Burchiello* (www.burchiello.it) motorboat, traces the lives of Venetian nobility in their summer villas; book through travel agencies. The return journey is by coach.

Chorus Churches: Chorus (www.chorusvenezia.org) promotes the preservation of the city's churches and offers guided tours from Mar–Jun and Sept–Dec to a number of churches. An unbeatable discount pass (€10) covers entrance to 15 Venetian churches, including the Frari, and may be bought at any of the participating churches. Charges go towards local church restoration projects.

Flights over Venice: the Aeroclub di Venezia at Aeroporto Nicelli airport on the Lido offers 6-30 minute long helicopter flights.

Lagoon tours: Destination Venice offer made-to-measure explorations of the lagoon and islands, along with individual guided walks, and Venetian-style rowing lessons. Campo San Luca, San Marco 4590, tel 041-528 3547, www.destination-venice.com.

St Mark's and the Doge's Palace: Free tours of the Basilica in summer, while the **Secret Itinerary** (Itinerari Segreti; booking essential on www.

palazzoducale.visitmuve.it) shows you the ins and outs of life at the Palazzo Ducale.

Health and medical care

EU residents: obtain an EHIC (European Health Insurance Card), available online at www.ehic.org.uk, which provides emergency medical/hospital *(ospedale)* treatment by reciprocal agreement.

For US citizens: if your private health insurance policy does not cover you while abroad (Medicare does not have coverage outside the US), be sure to take out a short-term policy before leaving home.

Medical emergencies: ask at your hotel if you need a doctor/dentist who speaks English. Your consulate (see page 123) should also have lists.

Many doctors at Venice's only hospital, S.S.Giovanni e Paola, next to San Zanipolo, speak English; tel: 041-529 4111 (and ask for *pronto soccorso* – A&E/casualty).

Mosquitoes: these are a big nuisance in Venice in the hot summer months. Make sure to pack some anti-mosquito sprays and/or plug-ins, as well as cream to soothe bites.

Pharmacies: *Farmacie* open in shopping hours and in turn for out of hours services; the address of the nearest open one is posted on all pharmacy doors.

The Punta della Dogana art gallery

I

Internet

Most good hotels will offer internet access (often charged) but a number of budget ones offer it free. The **WiFi access scheme** (www.veneziaunica.it) costs €5 for 24 hours, €15 for 72 hours, €20 for a week; check the signal works in your chosen spots before buying a package. Internet points come and go, and are very limited.

M

Media and listings

Print media

Newspapers and magazines *(giornali, riviste)*: you can find quality English-language newspapers at airports but in surprisingly few city-centre newsstands *(edicole)*, mostly around San Marco, and always with a delay of 24 hours. For those who read Italian, the local newspaper is *Il Gazzettino*.

Listings magazines

In Venice, the only reliable listings magazine is the bi-monthly *Shows & Events*, available from the city's tourist offices (charge), which includes opening times for the month, and details of all major exhibitions and events.

Venice's other listings magazine, including useful practical information, is *Un Ospite di Venezia* (available online in English at www.unospite divenezia.it), available only from main hotels.

Television and radio

The Italian state television network, RAI (Radio Televisione Italiana), broadcasts three main channels, which compete with multiple independent ones, which are mostly dire. All programmes are in Italian, including British and American feature films and imports, which are dubbed. Many hotels have cable connections for CNN Europe, CNBC and other channels that offer world news in English including BBC World and Sky. Most radio stations broadcast popular music. The BBC World Service can be picked up on shortwave.

Money

Currency. Italy's monetary unit is the euro (€), which is divided into 100 cents. Banknotes are available in denominations of 500, 200, 100, 50, 20, 10 and 5 euros. There are coins for 2 and 1 euro, and for 50, 20, 10, 5, 2 and 1 cents.

Currency exchange. *Bureau de change* offices *(cambi)* offer longer opening hours than banks (Travelex offices at Piazza San Marco and the airport are open all day daily). Both cambi and banks charge a commission. Banks generally offer higher exchange rates and lower commissions. Passports are usually required when changing money.

ATMs. Automatic currency-exchange

The Winged Lion, emblem of the city of Venice

machines (*bancomat*) are operated by most banks and provide a convenient way of taking out money. Independent (non-bank related) ATMs can also be found in the centre of town.

Credit cards and traveller's cheques. Most hotels, shops and restaurants take credit cards but some of the smaller bars and cafés only accept cash. If the card's sign is posted in the window of a business, they must accept it. Traveller's cheques are less readily acceptable, and you will usually get better value if you exchange them at a bank. Passports are needed when cashing traveller's cheques.

Opening hours

Banks. Hours are Monday–Friday 8.30am–1.30pm, 2.35–3.30pm.

Bars and restaurants. Some café-bars open for breakfast, but others do not open until around noon; the vast majority shut early, at around 10.30 or 11pm. Old-fashioned *bacari* (wine and tapas bars) in the Rialto area often close early (at around 9.30pm). Most restaurants close at least one day a week; some close for parts of August, January and early February.

Churches. The 16 Chorus Churches (see page 125) are open Mon–Sat 10am–5pm. The Frari is also open Sun 1–6pm. Other churches are normally open Mon–Sat from around 8am until noon and from 3 or 4pm–6 or 7pm.

Sunday openings vary, some are only open for morning services.

Museums and galleries. Some close one day a week (usually Monday), but otherwise open at 9 or 10am–6pm.

Shops. Open Monday to Saturday, 9 or 10am–1pm, and 3 or 4–7pm. Some shops open all day and even on Sunday, particularly in peak season.

Police

Although you rarely see them, Venice's police (*Polizia* or *Carabinieri*) function efficiently and are courteous. The emergency phone number is 112 or 113, which connects you to a switchboard and someone who speaks your language.

Post offices

The most convenient post offices are on the Rialto at Calle San Salvador 5106, San Marco (Mon–Fri 8.30am–7.10pm, Sat 8.30am-12.35pm), and at Lista di Spagna 233, Cannaregio, (Mon–Sat 8.30am–2pm). Postage stamps (*francobolli*) are sold at post offices and tobacconists (*tabacchi*), marked by a distinctive 'T' sign.

Public holidays

Banks, offices, most shops and museums close on public holidays (*giorni festivi*). When a major holiday falls on a Thursday or a Tuesday, there may be a *ponte* (bridge) to the weekend,

Portrait of the Four Tetrarchs, San Marco

meaning Friday or Monday is taken, too.

The most important holidays are:

1 January: Capodanno/ Primo dell'Anno

6 January: Epifania

25 April: Festa della Liberazione

1 May: Festa del Lavoro (Labour Day)

15 August: Ferragosto (Assumption)

1 November: Ognissanti (All Saints)

8 December: Immacolata Concezione (Immaculate Conception)

25 December: Natale (Christmas Day)

26 December: Santo Stefano (Boxing Day)

Moveable Pasquetta: (Easter Monday) The **Festa della Salute** (21 Nov) and the **Redentore** (third Sunday of July) are special Venetian holidays, when many shops close.

R

Religion

Although predominantly Roman Catholic, Venice has congregations of all the major religions (see list below).

Anglican. Church of St George, Campo San Vio, Dorsoduro.

Evangelical Lutheran. Campo Santi Apostoli, Cannaregio.

Greek Orthodox. Ponte dei Greci, Castello.

Jewish Synagogue. Campo del Ghetto Vecchio 1149, Cannaregio (tel: 041-715 359)

Roman Catholic. Basilica San Marco. Masses in Italian; confession in several languages in the summer.

S

Smoking

In 2005, smoking was banned in public enclosed spaces throughout Italy. Smokers can face a fine up to €275 for breaking this law.

T

Telephones

The country code for Italy is 39, and the area code for Venice is 041. You must dial the '041' prefix even when making local calls within the city. Note that smaller bars and businesses increasingly only have mobile numbers.

Telephone boxes. Italy has the highest proportion of mobile phone ownership in Europe and although phone boxes still exist few are still functioning. Those that do work use phone cards *(schede telefoniche)* bought from Telecom offices or credit cards.

Mobile phones. EU mobile (cell) phones can be used in Italy, but check compatibility or buy an Italian SIM card, available from any mobile phone shop, if you are staying for long. Major networks are offered by Telecom Italia (TIM), Vodafone and Wind.

International calls. Dial 00, followed by the country code (Australia +61, Ireland +353, New Zealand +64, South Africa +27, UK +44, US and Canada +1), then the area code (often minus the initial zero) then the number.

Churches abound in Venice   *Madonna dell'Oro church*

Time zone

Italy is an hour ahead of Greenwich Mean Time (GMT). From the last Sunday in March to the last Sunday in October, clocks go forward an hour.

Tipping

A service charge of 10 or 12 percent is often added to restaurant bills, so it is not necessary to tip extra – perhaps just round up the bill. However, it is normal to tip porters, tour guides and elderly gondoliers who help you into and out of your craft at landing stations.

Toilets

There are toilets *(toilette, gabinetti)*, usually of a reasonable standard but with a charge of €1.50, at the airport, station, in car parks and some main squares. It's cheaper to have a stand-up espresso at a bar and use their facilities. *Signori* means men; *signore* means women.

Tourist information

The best website is www.turismovenezia. it, the **Venice Tourist Board** site, which lists events, itineraries, excursions and hotels: There's also a call centre for visitors: tel: 041 24 24.

The Italian National Tourist Board (ENIT) offices abroad may provide basic information:

Australia Ground Floor, 140 William Street, East Sydney; tel: 02 9357 2561.
Canada 110 Yonge Street, Suite 503, Toronto, Ontario M5C 1T4. tel: 416-925 4882; www. italiantourism.com.
UK/Ireland 1 Princes Street, London W1B 2AY; tel: 020-7408 1254; www. enit.it.
US
Chicago: 500 N. Michigan Avenue, Suite 506 , Chicago, IL 60611; tel: 312-644 0996; www.italiantourism.com.
Los Angeles: 10850 Wilshire Boulevard, Suite 575, Los Angeles CA 90024; tel: 310-820 1898; www.italiantourism. com.
New York: 630 Fifth Avenue, Suite 1565, New York, NY 10111; tel: 212-245 5618; www.italiantourism.com.

Tourist information offices in Venice. The best tourist office (APT) is in the **Venice Pavilion** (tel: 041-529 8711) beside the Giardinetti Reali (Public Gardens). The hard-working but understaffed office is open daily 10am–7pm. There is an even busier office on the western corner of **Piazza San Marco**, opposite Museo Correr: San Marco 71/f, Calle dell'Ascensione/Procuratie Nuove; daily 9am–7pm. Both offices supply information, but most of it, even maps, events listings and other brochures, has to be paid for. They also offer booking for tours and events.

The tourist office at the railway station is also useful: **APT Venezia, Stazione Santa Lucia** (daily 8am– 6.30pm), as is the one at the airport: **APT Marco Polo** (daily 9.30am–7.30pm). This mostly deals with accommodation and transport tickets.

The train to Venice

Tourism passes

To keep costs down, and avoid queuing, it's worth pre-booking museum, church and transport passes, especially for St Mark's Basilica, the Doge's Palace and the Accademia. Attractions that must be pre-booked are the Clock Tower and the Secret Itineraries tour of the Doge's Palace (see page 125).

Venezia Unica (www.veneziaunica.it) is an online-only booking system for churches, museums, transport options and WiFi, with discounts offered in quieter periods to encourage sustainable tourism.

Hello Venezia (www.hellovenezia.it) is most useful as a transport and/or museum and eventbooking system and sells the **Venice Card**, which covers 12 museums and the 16 Chorus Churches (see page 125), and offers the full range of integrated transport passes for different times.

Rolling Venice. A youth pass for those between 14 and 29. For €4, it provides museum discounts, shopping, restaurant and hotel discounts, and a discounted 72-hour vaporetto pass for only €18. Sign up at the train station, or the ACTV office in Piazzale Roma.

Vivaticket (www.vivaticket.it; tel: 84 808 2000, Italy-only call centre) is a booking service for opera, concerts, ballet and blockbuster exhibitions, as well as major attractions and unusual guided tours, notably the Secret Itineraries tour and the Clock Tower.

The Chorus Pass (www.chorusvenezia. org) allows access to 16 Venetian churches (including the Frari), with charges going towards local church restoration projects (see page 125).

Transport

Getting to Venice

By air: Companies flying from the UK include British Airways (www.british airways.com) and EasyJet (www.easyjet. com). Ryanair (www.ryanair.com) runs regular flights from Stansted to Treviso airport (32km/20 miles from Venice) which is linked to the city by coach. From the US there are some direct flights from New York but most visitors come via Rome or Milan.

By train: Stazione Ferroviaria Santa Lucia is well-connected to Turin, Milan, Florence and Rome, as well as Paris and London. Travel via Eurostar/Thello, departing London 2.55pm and arriving in Venice at 9.30am the following day.

By car: please see Driving section (see page 122) – but don't arrive by car unless you really have to.

From the airport to Venice

Venice Marco Polo is Venice's main airport, on the edge of the lagoon, 13km (8 miles) north of the city centre. (tel: 041-260 9260; www.veniceairport.it).

Public bus No. 5 (ACTV, www.actv.it) runs from the airport to the bus terminus at Piazzale Roma every half-hour in summer and once an hour in winter; the blue airport buses (ATVO, www.atvo.it) have a similar timetable, journey time

Venice's Marco Polo airport

(30 mins) and price (€6 single). Buy tickets from the ATVO office in the arrivals terminal. A land taxi costs approximately €35. Once at Piazzale Roma, board the No. 1 vaporetto for an all-stages ride along the Grand Canal; take the No. 2, if you want the quickest route to San Marco. The Ponte de la Costituzione also connects by foot to the main train station.

The more dramatic entry to Venice is via the Alilaguna **public launch service:** (www.alilaguna.it), which connects Venice and the airport (from €30 return, but discounts if you buy online); key routes are Blue (Blu) to Zattere (1hr 40 mins) via Fondamente Nuove and San Marco 90 minutes and Orange (Arancio) to Santa Maria del Giglio (near San Marco, 72 mins) via the Rialto (1hr)

Private water taxis *(taxi acquei)*: the speediest and most stylish way to arrive (30 mins) but the priciest (around €110 to St Mark's) so don't confuse them with the Alilaguna craft. Taxis will take you to your hotel if it has a water entrance. For all water transport from the airport you have to walk about 500m/yds from the new terminal to the small docks.

Treviso is a small airport 32km (20 miles) north of Venice, used mainly by charters and low-cost airlines such as Ryanair, who call it 'Venice Treviso airport'. ATVO's Eurobus runs between Treviso and Piazzale Roma, (€18 return). The bus takes 45–70 minutes depending on traffic. Tickets can be bought in the airport or on board.

Getting around Venice

Venice is the only city in the world where the only form of public transport is some kind of boat. Once you have mastered a few key vaporetto routes, water transport is quite straightforward and certainly the best way to get around far-flung parts of the city. However, most of the time you will probably be walking, which is more practical for the city centre.

A timetable with water **transport map** is available free of charge from around a dozen Hello Venezia offices throughout the city, including the railway station and Piazzale Roma (tel: 041-24 24, www.hellovenezia.it). Alternatively check ferry routes on the public ACTV water transport site (www.actv.it), which is reliable for maps, timetables and ferry routes for the vaporetti (waterbuses).

Venezia Unica (www.veneziaunica.it) deals with integrated transport, including pre-booking transport and museum passes, WiFi and offers a good interactive map. The price you pay will differ according to the services you choose, the time of year and day of the week.

Pre-book a city transport pass (including islands), which is good value: €50 for 7 days, €35 for 3 days, €30 for 2 days, €25 for 36 hours, €20 for 24 hours; €7 for an hour's journey. Before every journey, swipe the card at the sensor by the

Transport Venetian-style

boarding pier: a green light and a bleep means the pass is valid; otherwise seek assistance. Failure to validate tickets may incur a fine.

Vaporetti (waterbuses): These workhorses will take you to within a short walk of anywhere you want to visit. The numbers and routes change fairly frequently but you can always depend on the romantic No. 1, which stops at every landing stage along the Grand Canal; No. 2 provides a faster service down the Grand Canal as part of its circular San Marco, Giudecca canal, Piazzale Roma route (and the Lido in summer). Nos 4.1 (anticlockwise) and 4.2 (clockwise) – formerly 41 and 42 – take a circular route, calling at San Zaccaria, Il Redentore, Piazzale Roma, the railway station, Fondamente Nuove, San Michele, Murano and Sant'Elena. Vaporetti Nos 5.1 and 5.2 – formerly 51 and 52 – also provide long, scenic, circular tours around the periphery, as well as stopping at Murano; in summer they go on to the Lido (change at Fondamente Nuove to do the whole route). Note that the circular routes travel up the Cannaregio canal, stopping at Guglie, and then skirting the northern shores of Venice. Nos 6 provides a fast route between Piazzale Roma and the Lido, going via the Zattere (Giudecca canal). For Burano, take No 12 from Fondamente Nuove via Murano. Line 9 connects Burano with Torcello. For the smaller islands, always double-check return times before setting out, as these ferries can be fairly infrequent and you don't want to be stranded.

The most confusing landing-stages are at Piazzale Roma, San Zaccaria (Riva degli Schiavoni), San Marco and Fondamente Nuove because they are spread out along the quaysides, with different services running from different jetties. The times displayed are generally reliable.

Gondolas: These are notoriously expensive but most visitors reckon they are worth the money. The city sets official rates, currently €80 for 40 minutes (up to six people), then €40 for each subsequent 20 minutes. The evening rate (from 7pm–8am) climbs to €100, then €50 for extra for every 20 minutes. However, some gondoliers will disregard the official rates or shorten your ride. Always agree a price and a route in advance (or get your hotel concierge to do it for you if you're willing to pay a commission). You can find gondolas at the main tourist areas, from Tronchetto and Piazzale Roma to the Rialto Bridge area, the Doge's Palace and at busy pedestrian crossings along the side-canals. Serenaded gondola tours lasting 40 minutes cost €44 per person, but as well as being expensive they are not authentic or traditional.

Water taxis *(motoscafi)*: A door-to-door service that comes at a high cost. One of the main stands is on the Riva degli Schiavoni, near San Marco.

Traghetti: The *traghetto* (gondola ferry, €2) operates at half a dozen key points

Ornate gondola   *A gondola selfie*

across the Grand Canal, saving a good deal of walking. It is customary (but not obligatory) to stand while crossing.

Walking: Venice is so compact that it is often quicker (and cheaper) to walk than to hop on a water bus. You need allow only 35 minutes to cross the city from north to south on foot – provided you do not lose your way. Most visitors do, and this is part of the fun of exploring. Official addresses, labelled by just the street number and sestiere (neighbourhood), are confusing. If in doubt, ask for the name of the closest church, square or nearest landmark; this is more helpful than the postal address.

W

Websites

A round-up of the city's key online sites, all mentioned earlier, that will help you plan your trip:

Transport and museums

ACTV Public water transport: maps, routes and timetables. www.actv.it.

HelloVenezia For booking integrated transport, ticketing and museums. www.hellovenezia.it.

Venezia Unica For integrated transport, ticketing and museums, including pre-booking transport and museum passes. Also a good interactive map of Venice. www.veneziaunica.it

Culture and events

Venice tourist board For what's on in Venice: events, itineraries, excursions, hotels. www.turismovenezia.it.

La Biennale Venice's arts jamboree, in uneven years. www.labiennale.org.

Venetian Club Crafts, cookery and Venetian-style rowing courses. www.thevenetianclub.co.uk.

Exploring and background

Venice in Peril Avoid its advice at your peril. www.veniceinperil.org.

MOSE flood barrier Detailed information and videos on the MOSE mobile barrier, being constructed to save Venice from flooding. www.mosevenezia.it.

Women

Venice is an extremely safe city, and arguably there is far less hassling and unwanted attention than anywhere else in Italy. Even late at night, catching ferries, or walking around Central Venice alone, Venice feels very unthreatening.

Y

Youth hostels

There are half a dozen youth hostels (*ostelli della gioventù*) in Venice (www.ostellidellagioventu.com). Particularly appealing is Generator (www.generatorhostels.com), Fondamenta delle Zitelle, Giudecca 86; tel: 041-877 8288, with sweeping views across to Venice. Unrecognisable from the former hostel, this converted grain warehouse has stylish public areas, more akin to a hotel than hostel, and a choice of private rooms or dormitories, including female-only dorms, all with comfy beds and modern bathrooms. Guests of all ages come here.

Direction signs are posted on the walls in Venice

LANGUAGE

Italian is relatively easy to pick up, if you have any knowledge of French or Spanish (or a grounding in Latin). Most hotels have staff who speak some English, and unless you go well off the beaten track, you should have little problem communicating in shops or restaurants. However, there are places not on the tourist circuit where you will have the chance to practise your Italian, and local people will think more of you for making an effort. Here are a few basics to help you get started.

Useful phrases

General
Yes *Sì*
No *No*
Thank you *Grazie*
Many thanks *Mille grazie/Tante grazie*
You're welcome *Prego*
All right/That's fine *Va bene*
Please *Per favore/Per cortesia*
Excuse me (to get attention) *Scusi*
Excuse me (in a crowd) *Permesso*
Could you help me? (formal) *Potrebbe aiutarmi?*
Certainly *Ma, certo/Certamente*
Can you show me...? *Può indicarmi...?*
Can you help me, please? *Può aiutarmi, per cortesia?*
I need... *Ho bisogno di...*
I'm lost *Mi sono perso*
I'm sorry *Mi dispiace*

I don't know *Non lo so*
I don't understand *Non capisco*
Do you speak English/French/Spanish? *Parla inglese/francese/spagnolo?*
Could you speak more slowly? *Può parlare più lentamente, per favore?*
Could you repeat that please? *Può ripetere, per piacere?*
How much does it cost? *quanto costa?*
this one/that one *questo/quello*
Have you got...? *Avete...?*

At a bar/restaurant
I'd like to book a table *Vorrei prenotare un tavolo*
Have you got a table for... *Avete un tavolo per...*
I have a reservation *Ho prenotato*
lunch *il pranzo*
supper *la cena*
I'm a vegetarian *Sono vegetariano/a*
May we have the menu? *Ci dia la carta?*
What would you like? *Che cosa prende?*
I'd like... *Vorrei...*
mineral water *acqua minerale*
fizzy/still *gasata/naturale*
a bottle of *una bottiglia di*
a glass of *un bicchieri di*
red wine *vino rosso*
white wine *vino bianco*
beer *una birra*

Numbers
One *uno*
Two *due*

Queue here for a gondola

Three *tre*
Four *quattro*
Five *cinque*
Six *sei*
Seven *sette*
Eight *otto*
Nine *nove*
Ten *dieci*
Twenty *venti*
Thirty *trenta*
Forty *quaranta*
Fifty *cinquanta*
One hundred *cento*
One thousand *mille*

Getting around
What time do you open/close? *A che ora apre/chiude?*
Closed for the holidays *Chiuso per ferie*
Where can I buy tickets? *Dove posso fare i biglietti?*
What time does the train leave? *A che ora parte il treno?*
Can you tell me where to get off? *Mi può dire dove devo scendere?*
Where is the nearest bank/hotel? *Dov'è la banca/l'albergo più vicino?*
On the right *a destra*
On the left *a sinistra*
Go straight on *Va sempre diritto*

Online
Where's an internet cafe? *Dov'è un Internet caffè?*
Does it have wireless internet? *C'è il wireless?*
What is the WiFi password? *Qual è la password Wi-Fi?*

Is the WiFi free? *Il WiFi è gratis?*
How do I turn the computer on/off? *Come si accende/spegne il computer?*
Can I...? *Posso...?*
access the internet *collegarmi (a Internet)*
check e-mail *controllare le e-mail*
print *stampare*
plug in/charge my laptop/iPhone/iPad? *collegare/ricaricare il mio portatile/iPhone/iPad?*
access Skype? *usare Skype?*
How much per hour/half hour? *Quanto costa per un'ora/mezz'ora?*
How do I...? *Come...?*
connect/disconnect *ci si collega/scollega*
log on/log off *si fa il login/logout*
What's your e-mail? *Qual è la sua e-mail?*
My e-mail is... *La mia e-mail è...*

Social media
Are you on Facebook/Twitter? *È su Facebook/Twitter? (polite form) Sei su Facebook/Twitter? (informal form)*
What's your user name? *Qual è il suo nome utente? (polite form) Qual è il tuo nome utente? (informal form)*
I'll add you as a friend. *La aggiungerò come amico. (polite form) Ti aggiungerò come amico. (informal form)*
I'll follow you on Twitter. *La seguirò su Twitter. (polite form) Ti seguirò su Twitter. (informal form)*
I'll put the pictures on Facebook/Twitter. *Metterò le foto su Facebook/Twitter.*

The Palazzo del Cinemà during the Venice Film Festival

BOOKS AND FILM

There is something about Venice that seems to get under writers' skins. A great number have lived and worked in the city, fallen in love with it, and made it the subject of novels and poems. Henry James may have put his finger on it when he said that 'everyone interesting, appealing, melancholy, memorable or odd' gravitated towards Venice.

Venice has served as the backdrop – if not the star – to countless films. It is the home of the world's oldest film festival, founded by Mussolini in 1932. For 10 days in late August/early September the city plays host to a huge cast of Hollywood and European stars, and the attendant paparazzi. Recently the festival has gone all out for Hollywood glitz, even if worthy art-house winners tend to triumph in the end. The festival is centred on the Palazzo del Cinemà, built in the 1930s in triumphant Fascist style. Most tickets go to the film and press industries but there are some tickets available to the general public. For information check www.labiennale.org.

Books

Childe Harold's Pilgrimage by Lord Byron (1818). Classic poetic epic.

The Stones of Venice by John Ruskin (1851–53). Influential book on the buildings of Venice, for serious lovers of architecture.

The Aspern Papers (1888) and ***The Wings of the Dove*** (1902), by Henry James. Evocative accounts from one of the greatest observers of Venice.

The Makers of Venice by Mrs Oliphant (1898). Quirky personal account of Venetian doges, travellers and painters.

Death in Venice by Thomas Mann (1912). Haunting tale of love and loss.

Venice Observed by Mary McCarthy (1961). Acerbic look at Venice from an intelligent observer.

The Comfort of Strangers by Ian McEwan (1981). An eerie, memorable novel, evocative of the city's melancholic charms.

Venice, Biography of a City by Christopher Hibbert (1988). A readable, informative survey of the city.

Venice by Jan Morris (1960). Purple prose meets anecdotal account. *The Venetian Empire: A Sea Voyage*, also by Morris, reconstructs the empire by travelling along the historic Venetian trade routes.

Dead Lagoon by Michael Dibdin (1994). A subtle detective story.

Friends in High Places by Donna Leon (2001). One of a gritty detective series set in Venice.

Miss Garnet's Angel by Sally Vickers (2001). Whimsical tale of an art trail in Venice.

Dirk Bogarde stars in Death in Venice (1971)

A Venetian Affair by Andrea di Robilant (2003). An appealing historical romance by an aristocratic Venetian.

The City of Falling Angels by John Berendt (2005). An intriguing inquiry into mysterious Venice and the lives of its modern residents.

Francesco's Venice by Francesco da Mosto, (2005). Beautifully illustrated history of the city, written by an enthusiastic descendant of the noble da Mosto family.

Venice by Peter Ackroyd's (2009). An erudite and evocative portrait of Venice.

Stabat Mater by Tiziana Scarpa (2011). Prize-winning story of a troubled violin-playing orphan inspired by Vivaldi.

Film

The Merchant of Venice. Al Pacino stars as Shylock and Jeremy Irons as Antonio in Michael Radford's acclaimed 2004 version of Shakespeare's tragic tale, set in 16th-century Venice.

Don't Look Now. Nicolas Roeg's chilling 1973 film starring Julie Christie and Donald Sutherland. Based on a short story by Daphne du Maurier, it is the tale of a couple who go to Venice while grieving over the death of their daughter.

Death in Venice. Based on Thomas Mann's 1912 novel, Luchino Visconti's 1971 film stars Dirk Bogarde as Gustav von Aschenbach, a composer who falls in love with a Polish boy while staying at the Lido's Hôtel des Bains.

Everyone Says I Love You. Directed by Woody Allen in 1996, this off-the-wall musical comedy featured many scenes set along the Grand Canal and in the city's backstreets.

The Talented Mr Ripley. Anthony Minghella's adaptation of the Patricia Highsmith novel – starring Matt Damon, Gwyneth Paltrow, Jude Law and Cate Blanchett – used Venice as a backdrop for its beautiful people.

Dangerous Beauty. This passionate film depicts the life of courtesan Veronica Franco and captures the atmosphere of Venice's heyday.

Blume in Love. This 1973 romantic comedy, starring George Segal and Susan Anspach, moves to Venice when Segal's lovesick lawyer character returns to the city where he spent his honeymoon six years earlier.

Venice/Venice. So good they named it twice... The film was not a big hit, however, although the plot – an American film director in Venice to promote his entry in the festival – makes good use of the city.

James Bond. The well-travelled Mr Bond pops up briefly in Venice in From Russia With Love (1963), manages to drive a gondola on land in Moonraker (1979), and has all kinds of Venetian adventures in the acclaimed 2006 Casino Royale.

The Tourist. Starring Angelina Jolie and Johnny Depp, the 2010 film did neither any favours but Venice, at least, came out of it well.

ABOUT THIS BOOK

This *Explore Guide* has been produced by the editors of Insight Guides, whose books have set the standard for visual travel guides since 1970. With top-quality photography and authoritative recommendations, these guidebooks bring you the very best routes and itineraries in the world's most exciting destinations.

BEST ROUTES

The routes in the book provide something to suit all budgets, tastes and trip lengths. As well as covering the destination's many classic attractions, the itineraries track lesser-known sights, and there are also ex-cursions for those who want to extend their visit outside the city. The routes embrace a range of interests, so whether you are an art fan, a gourmet, a history buff or have kids to entertain, you will find an option to suit.

We recommend reading the whole of a route before setting out. This should help you to familiarise yourself with it and enable you to plan where to stop for refreshments – options are shown in the 'Food and Drink' box at the end of each tour.

For our pick of the tours by theme, consult Recommended Routes for… (see pages 4–5).

INTRODUCTION

The routes are set in context by this introductory section, giving an overview of the destination to set the scene, plus background information on food and drink, shopping and more, while a succinct history timeline highlights the key events over the centuries.

DIRECTORY

Also supporting the routes is a Directory chapter, with a clearly organised A–Z of practical information, our pick of where to stay while you are there and select restaurant listings; these eateries complement the more low-key cafés and restaurants that feature within the routes and are intended to offer a wider choice for evening dining. Also included here are some nightlife listings, plus a handy language guide and our recommendations for books and films about the destination.

ABOUT THE AUTHORS

Italy specialist Susie Boulton has travelled extensively in the country for more than 30 years, written and contributed to many Insight titles and is the author of three guidebooks to Venice. Thanks also go to Jessica Stewart and Lisa Gerard-Sharp.

CONTACT THE EDITORS

We hope you find this Explore Guide useful, interesting and a pleasure to read. If you have any questions or feedback on the text, pictures or maps, please do let us know. If you have noticed any errors or outdated facts, or have suggestions for places to include on the routes, we would be delighted to hear from you. Please drop us an email at insight@apaguide.co.uk. Thanks!

CREDITS

Explore Venice
Contributors: Susie Boulton,
Lisa Gerard-Sharp
Commissioning Editor: Carine Tracanelli
Series Editor: Sarah Clark
Pictures/Art: Alice Earle/Shahid Mahmood
Map Production: original cartography
Berndtson & Berndtson, updated by Apa
Cartography Department
Production: Rebeka Davies
Photo credits: Alamy 4BC, 5MR, 22, 23,
25R, 24/25, 26ML, 31L, 32/33, 37, 47R,
49, 53, 54/55, 56, 62, 66, 67, 68, 84, 97,
104/105, 108, 137; Apa Publications 6MC,
6ML, 24, 26MC, 40, 50/51, 52, 65, 69,
75, 77L, 78, 79, 89, 92, 98, 127, 129R;
Bigstock 41L, 81, 107R, 115; Bridgeman
4MC; Britta Jaschinski/Apa Publications
100; Dreamstime 1, 2MC, 2ML, 2/3T,
6ML, 6MR, 9, 10/11, 11R, 12, 14, 15,
17R, 18, 20, 21, 28, 30, 34, 35R, 36,
38/39, 40/41, 42, 46, 46/47, 48, 50,
51R, 54, 57, 58/59, 59R, 60, 61, 63R, 64,
70/71, 72, 73R, 72/73, 74, 76, 76/77,
83R, 82/83, 86/87, 90, 90/91, 91R, 93,
94MC, 94MR, 94MR, 94ML, 94/95T, 103,
106/107, 110/111, 112, 116, 117, 118,
118/119, 120, 121, 123, 124, 125R,
128/129, 132, 132/133, 133R, 135, 136;
Getty Images 4ML, 5T, 5MR, 6/7T, 8, 10,
19, 26ML, 26MR, 26/27T, 29, 33R, 34/35,
43, 44/45, 62/63, 70, 86, 88; iStockphoto
2ML, 2MR, 2MR, 2MC, 4TL, 5M, 6MC, 6MR,
13L, 12/13, 16, 16/17, 26MC, 26MR,
30/31, 32, 55R, 58, 71R, 80, 82, 94ML,
94MC, 101, 102, 106, 109, 110, 111R,
113, 114, 119R, 122, 124/125, 126,
128, 130, 131, 134; Luna Baglioni 96, 99;
Photoshot 85, 87R
Cover credits: Front Cover Main: Santa
Maria della Salute, 4Corners Images
Front Cover BL: Carnival masks, iStockphoto
Back Cover (Left): Dorsoduro , Dreamstime
(Right): Burano, Dreamstime

Printed by CTPS – China

DISTRIBUTION

Worldwide
APA Publications GmbH & Co. Verlag KG
(Singapore branch)
7030 Ang Mo Kio Ave 5, 08-65
Northstar @ AMK, Singapore 569880
Email: apasin@singnet.com.sg
UK and Ireland
Dorling Kindersley Ltd (a Penguin Company)
80 Strand, London, WC2R 0RL, UK
Email: sales@uk.dk.com
US
Ingram Publisher Services
One Ingram Blvd, PO Box 3006, La Vergne,
TN 37086-1986
Email: ips@ingramcontent.com
Australia and New Zealand
Woodslane
10 Apollo St, Warriewood NSW 2102,
Australia
Email: info@woodslane.com.au

INDEX